MY KIND OF MAGIC

MY KIND OF MAGIC

Joyce Grenfell

A SCRAPBOOK

Compiled and introduced
by Janie Hampton

JOHN MURRAY

First published in Great Britain in 2004 by John Murray (Publishers)
A division of Hodder Headline

1 3 5 7 9 10 8 6 4 2

A CIP catalogue record for this title is available from the British Library

ISBN 0 7195 6633 9

Printed and bound by
Clays Ltd, St Ives plc

Hodder Headline policy is to use papers that are natural, renewable and recyclable products and made from wood grown in sustainable forests. The logging and manufacturing processes are expected to conform to the environmental regulations of the country of origin.

John Murray (Publishers)
338 Euston Road
London NW1 3BH

The jolly decent fair's fair dedication:
To Edna and Freddie who made the whole thing possible.

The Jocular:
To L.B.W. who said I'd never do it!

The unsentimental sentimental:
To my brother who is the one who really did it.

More jocular dedications:
To my family without whose assistance, encouragement and enthusiasm this book would have been written in half the time.

To George in spite of his threats.

To my readers, if any.

The Transatlantic slim volume:
To all who may read this little book I tender the hope they may be refreshed as they go on their way.

The casual reminding you of something deeper:
To remind you of Totnes. Eric.

These dedications come from a talk that Joyce gave with Stephen Potter at the first Cheltenham Literary Festival in 1949. In 'Hurray for Books', they satirised English literature and 'writership' – the art not only of impressing the public but of getting on top of both fellow authors and critics. 'A simple way to impress the public is by dedications, especially in Latin or better still, actual Greek,' they wrote.

Hereford.
1955.

Dear Joyce
To thank you for
Cheque, and it was
MOST generous of you
to add to it so, and
to wish yourself & Reggie
a very happy New Year. AND
to thank you for the Christmas card
which we all loved and which gave
great delight in the village where we
spent Christmas.
We all sat round on
Boxing day & listened to your broadcast
and loved it and I wondered where
you were listening to it.
I haven't yet heard
from the photographer, he is
a most elusive person & before
Christmas I'm sure every time I knocked

Letter from John Ward to Joyce, 1955

Contents

JOYCE OUT AND ABOUT

JOYCE ON MUSIC

JOYCE’S INSPIRATION

JOYCE’S FAVOURITE PLACES

Introduction

Throughout her life, Joyce Grenfell collected items that interested her such as theatre programmes, photographs and sheet music. She also filled notebooks with ideas for songs, sketches and radio talks, conversations that she overheard, drawings and poems – many of which have never been seen before. Her husband Reggie collected press cuttings, reviews and articles by and about her. She had always intended to collect this material into a scrapbook, but her life was so busy that she never had time. These are now brought together to remind us of the diversity of her interests and talents, both funny and serious. They are not in the order in which they were written, but themed into the subjects that interested her, such as friends, work and home.

'My Kind of Magic' was one of Joyce's favourite topics, which she wrote in several versions: as an article, a lecture and a radio talk. Here we have the article as it appeared in 1967, in which she described her friend the painter Mary Potter's 'magic touch with muted colours' and way of 'un-arranging' flowers.

From the start of the Second World War, Joyce appeared on the radio more often than any other woman in the twentieth century. Her first programmes included *Cocktails*, *Kippers and Capers*, *The Whoopee Club* and *Middle East Merry-Go-Round*, broadcast to troops overseas from the Paris Cinema in Lower Regent Street. After the war she made a series of songs and sketches called 'A Note with Music'. A few of the scripts have survived, still bearing Joyce's hallmark of acute social observation: Shirley's Girlfriend had the same trouble buying new shoes in 1947 as anyone might experience now.

Joyce's first collaborator on the radio was the legendary radio producer Stephen Potter, who later became famous for his *Gamesmanship* and *Oneupmanship* books. Between 1943 and 1955 they wrote and performed over twenty programmes in a series called *How*. These covered every subject from 'How to Give a Party' to 'How to Lead a Really Full Life'.

9.55 HOW TO LEAD A REALLY FULL LIFE I

including 'How Not To' and 'How, particularly, to do it in London'

by Stephen Potter
and Joyce Grenfell

Illustrated by Joyce Grenfell
Betty Hardy, Carleton Hobbs
Deryck Guyler, James McKechnie
Production by Stephen Potter
(BBC recording)

This is the first of a new series of three 'Hows'; the others are 'How To Cross The Atlantic First Class' and 'How To Know America Really Well.' Stephen Potter and Joyce Grenfell have both visited the United States earlier this year.

Radio Times
Aug 19, 1955

10.0 HOW TO KNOW AMERICA REALLY WELL III

by Stephen Potter
With interruptions by
Joyce Grenfell
and illustrations by experts
Production by Stephen Potter
and Leonard Cottrell
(BBC recording)

Sept 2, 1955

In 'How to Talk to Children' we are introduced to a modern nursery school, where children are encouraged to express themselves through free dance. This was the origin of George ('don't do that') and his little friends.

Joyce was an avid reader of the *Christian Science Monitor* and a regular contributor of articles about life in London for its mainly American readers. 'A Lovely Wet Day' conjures up the delights of a damp day in Chelsea. Joyce was born, brought up and lived most of her life in Chelsea, where she knew all types of people. She always travelled around London by bus – she liked listening to the passengers and talking to the conductors. In a radio talk she describes some of her favourite London characters, including stage door-keeper Joe Dockery who lived to be 96. He always claimed that his telegram to Agatha Christie for *The Mousetrap*'s first night in 1952 said, 'Have a good week!'

Long before Joyce admitted to the world that she was a Christian Scientist, she was broadcasting on BBC religious programmes. She wrote hundreds of 'serious' BBC radio talks between 1964 and 1979 for *Ten to Eight, Woman's Hour* and *Thought for Today*. Here we include some thought-provoking talks on humility, prayer and happiness – what is it?

Music was Joyce's chief pastime when she was not working. She played the piano a little, and listened to the radio and gramophone records a lot. At every opportunity she went to concerts – in the Albert Hall, or at the Aldeburgh Music

Festival. She found it difficult to choose her favourite music for *Desert Island Discs* in 1951 but, unlike most marooned celebrities, she had another opportunity in 1971.

In 1960 Joyce was surprised to be invited by the Postmaster-General to join the Pilkington Commission into Broadcasting. For two years she attended meetings all over Britain, with people connected with broadcasting from every walk of life. To keep herself awake during these interviews she sketched portraits of the people. Some of these appear in this book – a few are named, others are anonymous 'types'.

Peter Scott

T.S. Eliot

A sense of place was very important to Joyce. When on holiday her favourite place was by the sea. Her article 'The Sights and Sounds of Seasides Long Ago' evokes beautifully the timelessness of the seaside: the smell and feel of sand, combined with a historical setting. No longer do children have to endure Liberty bodices and flannel petticoats, all tucked into rubber paddling drawers. But they still run away from tiny waves and make holiday friends while collecting cowrie shells.

'Disappointment' was not a word in Joyce's vocabulary. Her eternal optimism shines through in all these examples, whether it be the pleasure of a rainy day or a cancelled weekend in the country. Joyce made people laugh about the Women's Institute right back in 1939, over sixty years before the same jokes appeared in the 2003 film *Calendar Girls*. Her observations of people are just as pertinent in the twenty-first century as they were back then.

Janie Hampton

Joyce in Cumbria, 1963

'MY KIND OF MAGIC'

By magic I don't mean abracadabra and fairy godmothers with wishes, nor do I mean witches and spells and funny goings on at séances.

I mean the heightened quality of certain, often quite small, experiences lit by unexplained excitement, powerful with innocence. It can come from looking closely at a shell, arriving at an unexpected view of the sea, hearing a phrase of music. Blake knew all about it:

> To see the world in a grain of sand,
> And a heaven in a wild flower,
> Hold infinity in the palm of your hand,
> And eternity in an hour.

(It is interesting that Blake should speak of *a* Heaven, because of course there are many, and sometimes heaven is *here*.)

Magic is far more potent now in middle age than when one was new. I suppose it is because one brings *more* to each experience. Magic is very nourishing.

Places induce it. East Anglia with its high skies and clear light; the bush in Australia where the green is grey-green, as ours is green green and Ireland's is *greener* green green. I get it particularly in a certain small valley in Cumberland. The first time I went there, having chosen the place to stay from an un-illustrated guide book with just an inch of unexaggerated prose, we drove across a high bare pass and as we came near it I *knew*, instantly - this is it! I said it out loud, too. It wasn't a discovery, it was recognition and I get it, unfailingly, every time I go back there. It's my spiritual home, and I take it out and look at it in my mind's eye from time to time.

Of course magic can happen anywhere. Even Birmingham, the wrong end of Edgware Road or bleak bits of Scotland - that's Place magic.

There are other kinds: light magic, weather magic and seasonal magic. Small signals sometimes, usually ahead of time. Blackbirds in January, for instance, or a blackberry in July. I'm usually in the middle of summer when I feel it. I had it at dusk in East Anglia lately, driving up a track between two huge fields of cereals. Barley and wheat, both pale as a child's straw hat and edged with misty blue scabious, poppies, camomile daisies, pinkish mallow, little yellow snapdragons and blue speedwell. Dusk is a good time, when all the colours become luminous, and glow by their own light in the greyness.

Autumn has a special magic, when there is a very clear light and suddenly everywhere looks spacious without leaves. It anticipates next spring and the birds think so too and sing again. And I like winter moonlight with sharp pencil shadows of trees and wire fences on a pale star-sapphire landscape, they give me a feeling.

It is possible, I think to have a nostalgia for a past one could not have known. The latish Victorian era is my time. I like to view it from the comfort of today. I like to savour selected bits of what can now be seen as a serene and orderly past. It *wasn't* of course, but magic selects what it wants to see and from our present chaos it can be made to seem a world of positive, rounded-off conclusions. Very restful, I also like its slow tempo. An escape? Yes. And why not?

Visually that age appeals to me, the clothes they wore, the furniture they lived with: I refuse to be psychological about the significance of flounces and frills covering chair legs, I share the Pre-Raphaelite passion for details, and nature in detail: the dedicated reproductions of a bird's wing, a wild rose, ivy, and the weight and quality of Victorian dress silks. Oh, and the sheerness of muslin and dimity and print.

Do you know those books made of thick creamy coloured pages with little drawings at the start and end of chapters? Exquisite little drawings of bryony and traveller's joy, of a robin's nest with eggs in it, and everything penned with loving care. There's a good smell to these books too; musty and mysterious. They usually have heavy bindings and embossed titles in gold, and are often deadly dull to read but lovely to handle and look at.

Then there's colour magic. That's nourishing if you like, so long as it is one's own palette. I can't abide relentless orange, the kind without mercy. I don't feel easy with cheap-knitting-wool Kelly green, purple, or fierce pillar box red except on pillar boxes or buses.

People's houses reflect their awareness of colour sense. I have a painter friend who has a really magic touch with *muted* colours. Her rooms are for thinking in. She has, too, an artless way with flowers that makes most arranged arrangements look like an abuse of privilege. Some field daisies and cow parsley in a pale yellow jug against a putty pink wall, with an added white hydrangea head - or two clashing geraniums in a glass, clashing so that they almost make a sound. Her taste rings my bell and has magic.

Listening to music has been the most constant, ever increasing and developing pleasure I know. When I was young I listened because I saw pictures or liked the rhythms. Certain music stirred me, made me cry, yearn, sigh, gloat, and wallow. I stood night after night at the Queen's Hall Proms from the age of fourteen, emoting and getting nourished. Later I began to hear what I was listening to, the wallowing decreased but the nourishment increased.

Walford Davies once told me that when he was a young student he went nightly to the Proms and he discovered that after a Wagner concert the journey from the Queen's Hall to Oxford Circus seemed to take for ever and he was worn out by the emotion he'd expended earlier. But on the nights when Beethoven or Bach or Mozart had been played he covered the distance in no time at all and was so refreshed he could have run all the way home.

I think flowers and music give me the most pleasure. Of flowers, white ones in particular. I like them so that they appear to have built-in light and green shadows. Very white roses. White lilac, not the forced feeble kind that flops almost at once, but the tough open-air one with clusters big as bunches of grapes and the last buds at the top still tight bright green. And the smell! It's the most romantic of all scents. Roses are for any time, lilac is for fleeting fancies! White Christmas roses, well, they're cream really; little button ranunculus with green middles; and best of all, wild white violets.

One of the best magic moments is the finding of the first white violet of the year. No year is complete until I find one. And a cowslip - the downy pink stem is very satisfactory and the flower smells the way honey tastes.

The third important annual find is a wild strawberry. It is best when you find a tiny scarlet fruit hanging from the same plant as a white strawberry flower.

The thing about my kind of magic is that it is ever present, and past experience of it can be taken out and looked at again: 'recollected in tranquillity', like poetry, any time anywhere.

Like all moments of revelations, magic is un*self*conscious, like happiness. Perhaps it is another word for happiness? When one is entirely happy, one is un*self*conscious, a divine experience: bliss!

JOYCE AT WORK

Working at her desk
in Elm Park Gardens

1788

G.K.P.–15060x200 11-41.

The Indian Radio & Cable Communications Co., Ltd.
BOMBAY

R1254 1944 DEC 8 PM 8 27

R792 LONDON 26 8 0948 =

JOYCE GRENFELL GREENS HOTEL BOMBAY =

DEAR JOYCE PERFECTLY ALRIGHT IF YOU RETURN
MARCH AS PLANNING DO OPERETTE BEFORE REVIEW
HAPPIEST POSSIBLE CHRISTMAS ALL LOVE
= NOEL COWARD +

INWARD CCT NBR	INITIALS	TIME RECD

Telegram to Joyce in India from Noel Coward inviting her to perform in Sigh No More, the first post-war revue which opened at the Piccadilly Theatre in August 1945.

Piccadilly
GERrard 4506·7
Nightly 6·30
Wed. & Sat. 2·30
Cyril Ritchard
Madge Elliott
Noel Coward's
Sigh No More
Mantovani
and his Orchestra
Joyce Grenfell
Graham Payn

Joyce on the radio

The first paid job that Joyce had, in 1937 when she was twenty-seven years old, was as the Observer's first radio reviewer. Under the heading 'Broadcasting' she wrote a weekly review of all that she had heard on the BBC's single wireless channel. She had no idea she was to become so well known on the radio herself. But you can hear her voice in these reviews. One of her first was for the coronation of George VI, when Princess Margaret was six years old.

BROADCASTING

THE CORONATION PROGRAMME

This was a great week for the Radio. The Coronation Broadcast was a triumph from start to finish. Listeners followed the procession against a background of continuous cheering. Schoolchildren were massed on the Embankment. Their high-pitched ovation rang out in contrast with more adult acclamations. In the Abbey the scene was admirably described. Thanks to the concise and helpful account, it was easy to visualise the ceremonies. I liked hearing that Princess Margaret, intent on seeing everything, rested her chin on the edge of the Royal Box. The music of the choirs, the orchestra, and the new organ were throughout magnificent. The entire broadcast came through brilliantly, a fine achievement for the BBC.

* * *

The King's Speech, in the evening, was a fitting climax to a wonderful day. There was real feeling in His Majesty's deep voice.

* * *

Dear Brutus is the first play by Sir James Barrie to be heard on the wireless. It was produced by Val Gielgud, who had adapted it for broadcasting. Wisely, he used no sound effects. A few bars of music seemed to drift into hearing and again to fade away. The effect was especially good, in the first act, where Dearth draws back the

The Observer

curtain to find the mysterious wood arrived outside the window. Music rose in eerie volume. The dream quality in the wood scene was enhanced by the leisurely tempo of Val Gielgud's production. The play was well cast. Richard Goolden gave Lob the balance of reality and immortality that left one wondering. Nova Pilbeam, in spite of a tendency to clip her words in the modern stage manner, made an enchanting Margaret. Her final cry after Dearth was moving. It was a clever idea to have the stage directions read by Lewis Casson. This clarified the action and gave us the opportunity of hearing some charming prose.

* * *

The BBC Coronation Revue was produced by Harry S. Pepper. As an extra waiter George Robey was in happy vein. Innocent surprise at the misconstruction of his remarks, the fruity chuckle, and that vocabulary of out-size words – all were in evidence. There are few laughs more infectious than Cicely Courtneidge's. Her vitality penetrates the air and loses nothing in transit.

* * *

Two bird programmes last week. Eric Parker talked about summer birds from a Surrey wood. In spite of the disturbance of a circling aeroplane, blackbird, robin, thrush and woodpecker gave fine recitals. This was an unusually successful nature programme. The commentators need not have worried at the absence of rare birds. It was enough that the commoners sang. And sing they did, gloriously. Facts from Eric Parker about migrants: I like knowing that the chiff-chaff's other name is Little Jolly Sixpence.

16 May 1937

'Filling the stage'

by J.C. Trewin

Author of many books on the theatre, John Courtney Trewin was 'the performers' theatre critic' and much admired by Joyce. This review from the Illustrated London News of 1957 captures the flavour and memory of a whole evening's performance by Joyce at the Lyric Hammersmith.

MISS GRENFELL can summon hosts of friends. In her programme called 'A Miscellany' at the Lyric, Hammersmith, this artist creates her silent characters as vividly as the speaking ones. There is the pianist who must receive members of his public after the recital. We can easily imagine him as he stands, pale, polite, monosyllabic, surrounded by patronising Philistines, well-meaning dead-heads, and hearty morons, and waits until the last visitor has gone, to jump upon his hat, or smash the nearest window. Miss Grenfell does not take us to this exciting conclusion; but I think most of us know it is bound to come.

Then there is the family about to emigrate. We are at Waterloo Station. The mother-and-grandmother, left behind, is saying good-bye, determinedly cheerful. Nothing comic here: Miss Grenfell snatches us suddenly to the edge of tears. All loneliness is in her last slow walk away after the train has gone. It is the only time the artist turns her back on us, and expressive it is. Miss Grenfell, in the first minutes of her evening, can bring up to three complete companies: the bang-at-it seaside-pierrot type, the sophisticated-parochial, and, best of all, the battered more-or-less-Continental-type production in which a variety of 'fairly disinterested ladies' stand around, singing with disdain. It is worth the journey to Hammersmith to hear Miss Grenfell as she chants 'Fiesta! Fiesta!' in tones of modified rapture.

Much more yet. We have an entire North-of-England village committee, seen only through the eyes of the madam chairman. The task here is to get rid of the one unsuitable voice in the choir before the next Music Festival. It is a pity that the owner of the voice should also be the founder of the choir, but these things do happen. Miss Grenfell, her speech honed to the gleaming sharpness of an executioner's axe, flashes at the committee about her, and we feel more than a little sorry for May, the incompetent secretary, who seems to muddle everything she touches.

Presently we have moved to a nursery school where 'Free-activity' means half an hour of turmoil with the tots. At once the Lyric stage is crowded with the little angels, particularly George who appears always to be doing what he shouldn't, and Hazel who has her finger in the keyhole, like the Dutch child who plugged the dyke. Miss Grenfell contrives to be professionally caressing and practically distraught within the space of a few syllables. But then, she can manage this throughout the evening. When, at last, she takes a call in a black dress ('Makes a change,' she murmurs, after having appeared earlier in turquoise, flame, and lemon), the stage in front of the plain red drapes is crowded for us with concert-goers, choristers, revue artists, committee-women, and infants, not to speak of various television camera-men, the friend-to-tea, and the Teddy-boy on the Big Wheel.

I had better explain about these. The camera-men are watching the dim, but hopeful chatelaine who conducts viewers of her Stately Home (complete with bewildering architecture, Oliver Cromwell's button, thirty seven pictures of hollyhocks, and a temperamental echo). Elsewhere, the friend-to-tea, poor soul, can barely slide in a word because her hostess is so bothered about the iron in the kitchen, the picture awry on the wall, and the state of the cushions. Well-meant, certainly, but distracting. I shall not lose the moment when, her eyes lighthouse-bright with simulated interested, Miss Grenfell says 'How *is* poor Ethel? I was terribly worried when I heard she was tap-dancing again... Here's a pretty box, made by a Zulu.'

I have not forgotten the Teddy-boy on the Big Wheel. When the Wheel sticks, he and Shirl's girlfriend are aloft together, but Shirl's girlfriend does not find him an enthralling talker. Still, his companion has a properly crushing reply. 'Ta for the chat' she says with disdain. And 'Ta for the chat' we say to Miss Grenfell. It is an enchanting programme because she knows how far enchantment can stretch. When it begins to fray, she stops (unlike Beethoven, according to one of her concert morons: 'He does go on so').

Miss Grenfell's chief qualities are her gift of swift, witty exaggeration (an acute eye and ear behind it) and her natural kindliness. She does not make gargoyles of her people. As one of her Cockney women says, they are 'ever so inter*est*ing,' and always 'nice'. Professionalism does not obtrude: this is entertainment at a party where we are friends together. The sentiment may be perilous, but (as in 'Boat Train') it can come through, thanks to the artist's honesty.

Miss Grenfell, with her fringe, her bright eyes, her mobile mouth, and her untiring eagerness, can do as she wishes with an audience for nearly two hours.

Stage Requirements for Tour of North America, 1956

Joyce took her work very seriously. She believed that an audience expected the best you could give, and therefore she took great care to ensure that she was well rehearsed, well rested and the stage was well managed.

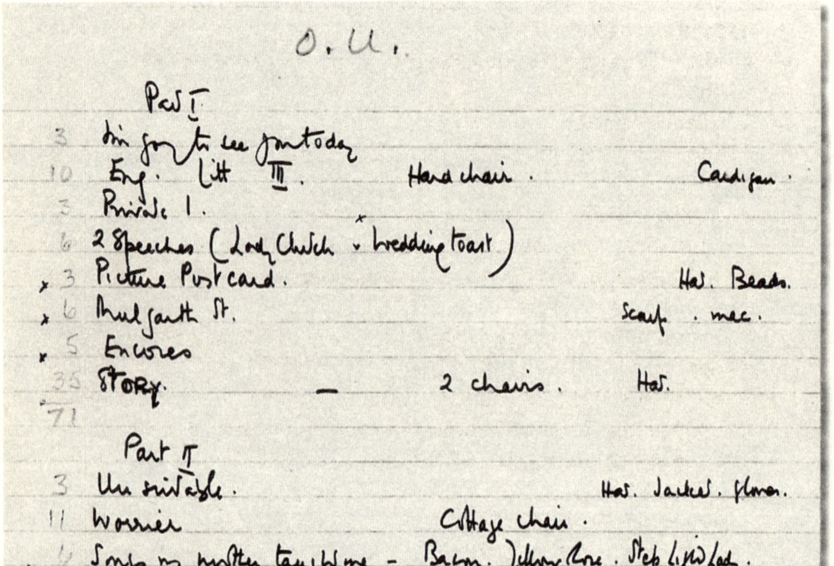

O.U.

Part I

3 I'm going to see you today
10 Eng. Litt III. Hard chair. Cardigan.
3 Private 1.
6 2 Speeches (Lady Church × Wedding toast)
x 3 Picture Postcard. Hat. Beads.
x 6 Mulgarth St. Scarf. mac.
x 5 Encores
35 Story. — 2 chairs. Hat.
71

Part II

3 Unsuitable. Hat. Jacket. flowers.
11 Worrier Cottage chair.
x 6 Songs my mother taught me – Basin. Yellow Rose. Step Lightly Lady.
x 5 ~~First Flight.~~ Life Story Hard chair.
Bill.
x 4 ~~Old Girls School Reunion~~ American Mother Hat?
x 5 Duet (Freda & Eric)
5 Nursery School.
x 3 Green Time.
54

—

x means not previously done at Wavendon.

Notes by Joyce for the running order of one of her shows

She created the setting through her monologues and songs, but she did require some basic furniture and the correct lighting. Her stage gowns were made of many yards of gathered silk, so needed considerable care in their ironing. Before she went on a tour she sent these stage requirements to each theatre and was not amused if they were ignored!

STAGE - back curtains and matching legs (use most attractive drapes available.) Gray or black satisfactory.

ON STAGE - Grand Piano (Steinway preferred) stage, right.

1 piano stool.

Piano _must_ be properly tuned on day of performance.

FURNITURE

1 plain chair; 1 small table, must be practical height for use as writing table, etc and light enough to be moved to various positions by Miss Grenfell.

1 other small table (card table will do) for use as prop table behind piano.

1 more decorative chair (possibly upholstered, but _not_ heavy) no arms, but back high enough for Miss Grenfell to lean on if sitting on it back to front.

1 low stool or pouffe.

1 hat stand (old fashioned type).

OFF STAGE

Two dressing rooms will be required. One (nearest to stage) for Miss Grenfell, and another for her accompanist.

LIGHTING

We will use whatever lighting facilities you have available. If you have balcony or front-of-the-house spots, these should be focused to give the stage a warm, overall light. (Use flesh pink gelatins _NO AMBER_.)

IMPORTANT

Please make arrangements to have a qualified woman available at the theatre at least _two hours_ prior to performance to press Miss Grenfell's four gowns.

'Laughing'

Laughter was the meat and bread of Joyce's work. This talk was written by Joyce for Woman's Hour on the BBC Home Service in 1953.

I don't think there is anything to equal the pleasure of laughing, I mean the sort of laughing you do when you are so delighted that you just give up and abandon yourself to it with your head thrown back and your feet at ease. It takes people differently of course. I've got an American friend who just shakes quite silently while tears spurt out of her eyes; and I know an enormous, tall dark man whose shoulders go up and down in a steady rhythm while he snorts in a terrifying way and frightens everyone around him. Another of my friends makes a noise rather like a boastful hen and another one barks.

But what I'd like to know is *what* makes us laugh? I suppose it can all be boiled down and analysed and I suppose its got something to do with a sense of proportion and the distortion of the ordinary - I don't know the rules - I only know that when the necessary combination is arrived at - hooray - I, and the rest of the world, have the wonderful pleasure of laughing. And, 'I always say a good laugh does you good.'

Christopher Fry in *The Lady's Not for Burning* makes one of his characters say 'Laughter is the surest touch of genius in creation. Would you ever have thought of it, I ask you, if you'd been creating man.'

The first time I ever played to an audience was a charity dress rehearsal of Herbert Farjeon's *Little Revue*. For some reason I thought that the *first night* was the really important one so this dress rehearsal didn't worry me very much. All I'd been afraid of was not remembering the words, I'd said them on buses, in the bath, walking down the street, to my husband. It was the one about the Women's Institute lecture and how to make boutonnières for the lapel from beech nut husk clusters and from the moment I began it, the audience laughed. It was the most astonishing sound I had ever heard and quite the most intoxicating. I couldn't believe it. *I* thought the monologue was funny - that's why I'd written it - but it had never occurred to me that it could do this. I felt the most extraordinary mixture of power and humility - all at the same time. Power because it seemed that I could make the audience do what I meant it to do and humility because, at the same time, it seemed to have nothing to do with me. I have never quite had that feeling so clearly since then. It was so very unexpected because I hadn't ever imagined the *sound* or the *feeling* of making people laugh.

I never get over the exciting feeling you get when you say something to an audience and a great wave of sudden laughter rises up at you. Nowadays a new thing happens to me sometimes. If there is someone in the audience with one of those infectious gurgling sort of laughs I get terrible internal giggles and want to laugh too - and I have to concentrate like mad on what I'm saying so as not to join in.

Of course giggling is another pleasure, there's nothing like it, is there? Other people's giggles are no fun at all and when actors giggle over private jokes on the stage it's bad manners and inexcusable but it's difficult sometimes not to do it. The slightest thing sets you off - as it does in church or anywhere else when it is a mistake for such a thing to happen. In *Penny Plain*, the revue I'm currently in, we have a trio of ladies singing in a choir at the Albert Hall. It looks pretty funny I believe - we're all in those white dresses, and we begin simply singing: 'Three lady choristers.' For some unknown reason the other night I chose to sing very loudly and very clearly, 'Three lady foresters.' It's not in the least funny really but of course it set us all off and just about finished Moyra Fraser. She was reduced to complete silence for several bars and just stood there making small moaning noises which didn't do anything to help the situation. We did pull ourselves together eventually - by thinking of sad things is one method - because we know how rude it was to the audience.

Children laughing are a very good sight. I like it when they get quite helpless and fling themselves down on the floor to finish it off that way. Such curious things set them off. I used to find the nursery rhyme line 'Old Mother Slipper-Slopper jumped out of bed' the funniest thing in the world. Slipper-Slopper was the key. And then one day I thought of Slipper-Slopper and it didn't work any more. I remember quite plainly the sense of disappointment.

People are funny about laughing and some even think it is a weakness to be ashamed of. A woman I know came to see a revue I was in and when it was over she said very apologetically, 'I couldn't help laughing.' What on earth, I wondered, did she think we were all doing working our heads off for out there on the stage?

Being funny is inexplicable - you either are or you aren't. All comics must think they are funny or they wouldn't go to all that trouble but it is fatal to *try* to be funny. I think you have to appear not to know you are doing it.

Having a reputation for being funny can be rather a heavy load to carry. My heart sank like a stone when I went to open a bazaar and the kindly intentioned lady who met me at the door said, 'You will make us laugh, won't you?'

It seemed a ghastly order at eleven in the morning. For the record I did just manage it. The old circus horse in me sniffed the sawdust, saw the audience and waded in.

I think laughing, like music, is an international language and I wish we all spoke it more.

Joyce and young fans, 1960

Overheards

'Overheards' were the raw material for Joyce's monologues and songs. Here are some of her favourites, collected from notebooks and letters.

An overheard that rings the bell, arrives whole and unexpected, without a lead-in or a follow-on to blur its crystalline perfection. This one rates high:

'He never noticed anything funny about her, except she liked to play the piano nude.'

She found the best overheards among unknown people, when she was not involved in the conversation. In a hotel in Edinburgh she noticed:

Three rugged Scottish ladies in their late sixties overpowering a small table covered in scones. The chief lady wore an entire cock's wing in her hat. They were having a happy time discussing illnesses. The lady in the hat leaned forward and said, 'You know what the vairduct was?' She paused for drama and added, 'Exhustion.'

Her smaller friend said, 'There's one thing, you don't die of exhustion.' The leader fixed her with a beady eye, 'You do if it goes on long enough.'

In a Belfast hotel she met a commercial traveller who revealed he had not married. He asked the passing waitress if he should do so.

'Well now,' she replied. 'It's a good idea, with the winter coming on.'

In a field near Dublin she listened to a farmer contemplating a horse that might leap out over the fence.

'No,' decided the farmer, 'he will not. Except he might.'

After attending a very modern opera she overheard a precious young man.

'Of course it's entirely divorced from . . . well, I don't quite know *what* it's divorced from.'

After an evening performance she peered into the looking-glass as she took off her make-up.

'I look just like a horse.' My dresser thought for a while before she said encouragingly, 'Well you haven't a horse's nostrils.'

In an RAF mess during the war, a woman was looking for her friends.

'Where are the others?' she asked. A Belgian pilot replied, 'The big pieces have gone on in advance.'

In a modern picture gallery a woman said:

'That shows what he could do when he was tired. He *was* tired, wasn't he?'

Joyce had a strict moral code about eavesdropping on the telephone. She could listen to strangers all day, but never listened in to people whose voices she recognised – she might have heard something she would rather not.

It is the mystery of segments of overheard conversations that I especially enjoy. 'My brother was a nun, you know,' became part of a monologue.

Her favourite shot past her in a bus queue:

'I said to her, Gladys, you'll never hold him with a string of beads.'

This mystery also applied to written notes. She used to stay at a house where a very deaf Bishop and his wife visited. Before the days of hearing-aids, they communicated with each other in writing. After they left, the family would gather up all the notes and try to reassemble them into order. No context could be found for:

'No darling, not hassocks, cold mutton.'

The job of taking telephone messages was ripe for misunderstanding. One day the Grenfells' Odd Man (who carried coals, cleaned boots, fetched cabs and did all the odd jobs that no other servant would do) left a note on the hall table by the phone.

'Lady Bilke is sorry she can.'

Nobody in the family had ever heard of Lady Bilke.

The Origins of 'George, Don't Do That'

One of Joyce Grenfell's favourite characters was George, the boy who later appeared in half a dozen monologues set in a nursery school. We, the audience, never saw him, but we could imagine just what he looked like and what he might be doing that he shouldn't ought to have.

Joyce always claimed that she had never set foot in a nursery school before she wrote her first 'Nursery School' monologue in 1945. In fact she was at the opening of Britain's very first state nursery school in Slough, in 1936. Her aunt, Lady Nancy Astor, believed that universal nursery education would prevent all future wars. After paying for its construction she persuaded the local authority to run it, and Joyce to work as a volunteer.

Joyce's nursery school first appeared on the radio in 1943. 'How to talk to Children' (with illustrative examples which include 'How Not to', and 'How They Used to'), included a discussion of 'The Modern Approach to Freedom of Expression'. The mutinous

Joyce at a nursery school in Oldham, Lancashire, 1955

Sidney made his world debut wishing to be a dancing horse. George was in the original script but was cut before transmission. Between 1945 and 1962 Joyce wrote seven nursery school sketches. Over the years, the children's names changed to suit the prevailing fashions – Wendy and Neville gave way to Shirleen and Elvis. But Sidney was always Sidney. Here is the original inspiration which Joyce wrote with Stephen Potter in 1943.

Now remember, children, dancing is the poetry of motion. Ready?

Spread out children - wider - wider - make a lovely fairy ring and we'll all be different flowers growing in the grass, shall we?

Now what are you going to be, Lavinia?

A bluebell, good. And Peggy? A pink rose - that'll be lovely. What is Neville going to be? A blackberry! Well not exactly a flower but never mind.

Joan?

Honeysuckle. Good.

Sidney? Sidney, pay attention dear, what flower are you going to choose to be? A horse isn't a flower, Sidney.

No, children, that isn't funny, it's very silly. If Sidney can't think of a flower we'll go on to someone else till he makes up his mind.

Susan? Another rose - perhaps you are a red one if Peggy is going to be a pink one? Good.

Now then, Sidney? No dear, a carrot isn't a flower either, think, Sidney - and don't blow like that dear.

A holly leaf. Well, all right if you can't think of anything better but it's not a flower is it?

What about a tulip? You'd rather be a holly leaf. All right then.

Now when Miss Bartle plays her music I want you to dance around the fairy ring up on the tips of your toes, light as feathers and remember you are all flowers.

St Trinian's and All That
Joyce on Film

Much to her annoyance Joyce became, and remains, most famous for the parts she played in over twenty films. She was usually cast as awkward, galumphing, unattractive women of the jolly-hockey stick variety. She longed to have more parts like the one she got in The Million Pound Note as the Duchess of Cromarty, with handsome Gregory Peck.

Joyce loses her heart to Terry Thomas in
Blue Murder at St Trinian's, 1957

I have come to believe that receiving and giving are really the same.

Giving and *receiving,* not giving and taking.

The receiver contributes his acceptance to what the giver is offering.

Two halves of a whole.

When there is an equal division of labour in theatre, the entertainer's ideas and the audience's imagination converge into one concept.

Then programmes work.

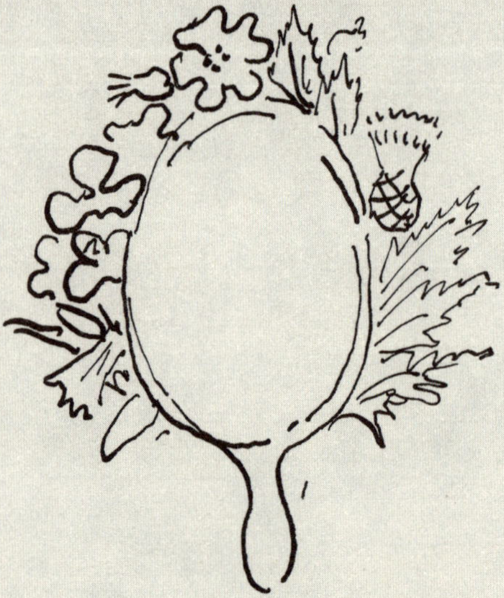

JOYCE AT HOME

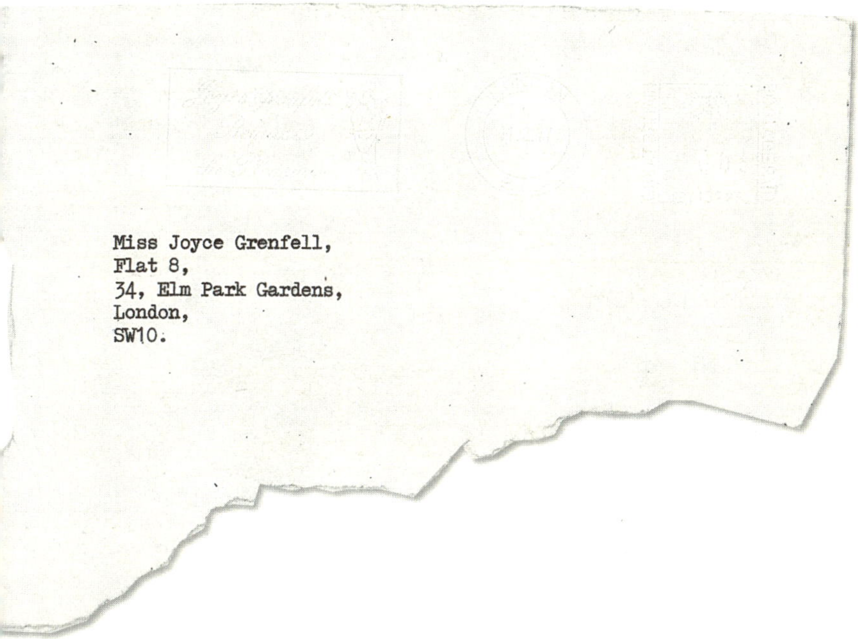
Miss Joyce Grenfell,
Flat 8,
34, Elm Park Gardens,
London,
SW10.

This appeared in the Daily Telegraph in 1954

WRITING IN THE KITCHEN

Like most women, actress Joyce Grenfell uses her kitchen as a workshop. Unlike most women, the work she does there is not cooking, washing-up and menu planning. It is writing.

The white topped table in her spacious kitchen-cum-dining room is the 'desk' at which she writes the material for her character sketches. For three months last summer she sat at her kitchen table every morning until 1 p.m. planning and writing lyrics and sketches for her show, **Joyce Grenfell Requests the Pleasure,** ***which opens in the West End tonight.***

SHE COOKS BY COMPULSION

Does she ever use her kitchen in a more orthodox way? 'Yes, but only when I have to,' she admits. A refreshing confession from an actress today when domesticity for stage personalities is fashionable.

She has her own ideas about other current customs. She prefers to write letters rather than have telephone chats, and gets through about ten shillings worth of $2\frac{1}{2}$d stamps a week doing it; likes small dinner parties where you can sit around and talk instead of large cocktail parties where you have to stand and shout; and would rather go to a concert or listen to her gramophone than watch TV. Her home is a two-floored flat high above a toy-shop in Chelsea's King's Road – she prefers to live in London, in spite of its smoke and grime.

Winifred Carr

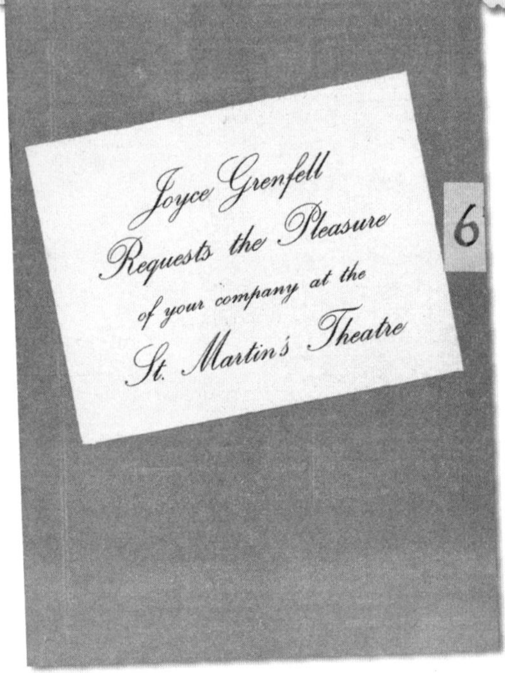

'My Idea of Comfort'

Home was very important to Joyce, her sanctuary away from the public life of theatre and celebrity parties. She wrote this article for Housewife magazine in 1954, when she lived with Reggie in the King's Road, Chelsea. After the war they always lived in small flats, but Joyce made sure they were welcoming and light, with plenty of fresh flowers.

Warmth, no draughts of any description; no overhead lighting except in the bathroom; hot water all the year round, and no noises about it being 'the summer'; pictures in the smallest room, if you like, but no literature. I'm not very fond of easy chairs. As I do all my writing on my knee, usually on a hard-backed *Radio Times* cover, what I really like is my own special corner of the sofa and all the rest of the sofa for my papers and gear.

I like small houses and small rooms with everything, as far as possible, literally within arm's reach. I simply don't want to live in rooms where you have to get up every time you want to turn on the radio or put on gramophone records.

For meals a kitchen-

Decorated envelope from John Ward

dining room is the answer to everything. My own is a perpetual joy – two walls are a kitchen and the other two are a very pretty leaf-green dining-room.

A new and heavenly comfort to me is the foam rubber mattress given to me as a first night present by my husband, it makes me feel as though I were being carried kindly all through the night. I like a low table beside my bed, with a drawer in it, a telephone and a switch to cut it off.

Life is so strenuous nowadays that I don't really want to take the lid off anything I needn't, so for sheer self-indulgence I like – close to hand – a large bowl of wrapped hard sweets when I'm working at home.

Joyce's two main comforts:
Reggie (left) and tennis

'Innings'

During the 1950s Joyce wrote for many magazines on domestic subjects such as 'Eating Habits', 'On Buying a Dress' or 'The Art of Not Being Bored'. This article about Innings appeared in Everywoman magazine in 1952.

ONE of the most delightful events is an Inning, as opposed to an Outing. An Inning is as beneficial to heart, feet and spirit as an Outing and in some of our lives it so rare that when it happens it is over before we have had time to savour its passing.

For a lot of people, particularly mothers with young children, Innings just aren't possible, for the ideal Inning is a complete withdrawal from society for at least eight hours, preferably to bed, with no duties to be attended to.

Slave all night the night before if necessary, write all those letters, darn, cook, trim a hat, but on the great Inning Day no 'oughts' must come into the picture. Solitude is imperative. I just doze most of the time and listen to the radio, but mostly I doze.

Ruth Draper does a monologue called 'A Quiet Morning in Bed' that illustrates how difficult it is to achieve an Inning. Her heroine was created in the spacious days when ladies not only had so-called leisure but also cooks to interview, French maids to give orders to, children's nurses to see, the little ones themselves to be kissed on their way to school, dentist and dancing lessons.

There were Italian ladies calling to give instruction on Dante while a manicurist gave attention to nails. We may never have experienced any of these trials but we smile and understand the joke.

For we, too, have our difficulties. There we are, lying back on our beds, having heard the front door shut behind our husbands and children, and we look at the whole beautiful, empty Innings day ahead of us and sigh with gratitude. Then it begins.

The tradesmen, for whom we have left a series of little notes in milk bottles and pinned to shopping bags hung on the back door, don't understand the notes or can't read. Anyway the bell goes.

Then a party carrying a notebook arrives with a petition but we see her from the bedroom window and ignore her rings. The postman brings an envelope that won't go through the letter-box. He knocks. It is an advertisement. None of this makes for peace.

The point of an Inning is its rarity. It is no good overdoing it. A variation on the idle Inning is the active one. I write from the point of view of one who never has time to sit and sew, or stand and cook except in short spurts, therefore a whole day of making Christmas cards or stitching a petticoat is a luxury.

It must be a left-over from childhood, when the school year began in September, that we still plan and start afresh then as at no other time of year, including January the first. I see it all so clearly on those fresh autumnal mornings and can't wait to get out of my cottons and into my wools and start the programme. Oh, the books I will read, the dishes I will cook, the poems I will write, the songs I will learn, and the Christmas presents I will make…

(There is also pleasure to be got from *not* going away, particularly in winter. The most perfect way to enjoy this is to be dreading – in a mild way, either through laziness or fear of boredom, or both – a weekend in a house we suspect of being cold. And then, on the very day itself, we are put off by our hosts because of a burst boiler or some other good reason.

It is like being given a beautiful present. Two whole days, Saturday and Sunday, given back to us full of glorious emptiness to fill as we fancy! There are few pleasures to be compared with the unexpected gift of space.)

In my teens the idea of an Inning would have meant nothing to me. Outings were all, every lighted candle called to my heart and my feet. But now it has got to be a whole chandelier full of flowering lights or the attractions of near and dear friends to lure me out of my rut. And Innings, those rare jewels, have an appeal that calls as loudly as the lighted candle once did.

Some sort of Puritan strain prevents most of us indulging in Innings even when opportunities arise. We feel we 'oughtn't'. Why? The result of a small withdrawal is sure to be a much nicer, kinder, fresher person and this benefits the world. But there it is, we are not yet very wise and we feel there is some virtue in carrying on till we fall down.

Don't look now but I think I've got an Inning creeping up before me for tomorrow, and that is why I am typing this article sometime after midnight to make space for it.

Joyce's Favourite Recipes

Although Joyce employed a housekeeper who did all her shopping and most of her cooking, she liked to cook for special occasions. Her favourite recipes reflected the tastes of the time – just emerging from rationing, when to get within a hundred yards of garlic was considered 'continental'. After Reggie gave her a food blender for Christmas, she became mad about making soup. She had planned to write a soup-recipe book one day. Here are some of her favourite recipes. They are hardly adventurous, but they catch the flavour of the 1950s and 60s.

Home made soup

Fry two slices of bacon. Add two pints of water, a stock cube, sliced onion, carrot, potato and two sticks of celery. Simmer for half an hour. Put into blender and season with salt and pepper.

Small squares of toast can be served with vegetable or meat soups

Peel, scald and slice the onions, and cook them lightly in the melted butter for ½ hour.

Special-occasion Soup
Heat up a tin of Fortnum & Mason's consommé and add a small glass of sherry before serving.

Summer Salad
Slice a cucumber wafer thin and soak in milk for an hour. Pour off milk and season.

Winter Salad
Chop up celery, apple and spring onions and mix with walnuts. Mix with a ready made mayonnaise.

Boxing Day Dessert
Take a can of apricots and put a teaspoonful of rather thick bitter marmalade in each apricot. Put on a baking tin and heat in the oven. Serve with coffee ice cream.

When Joyce got home from the theatre after an evening performance, her favourite food was steaming porridge with sugar and hot milk.

'I like it better than anything,' she said in 1955.

'A Lovely Wet Day'

When I was about eight years old we were seldom given a good long run at doing our own thing: piano practice, school homework, meals and being sent out in the nice fresh air interrupted our self-chosen activities. But an all-wet afternoon, with the rain settling in for a proper spell, presented us with a blank page of time to be written on in our own way; a bonus of space instead of the afternoon spent out of doors.

In those days I was an indoor girl. I had not yet discovered nature or tennis. On an all-wet afternoon I could do what I fancied most – draw and paint, dress up in my mother's hats and shoes and, sometimes, make fudge.

We were London children and lived in a flat without a garden or a balcony. Instead we had the narrow corridor that ran the length of the flat and that is where we played. By the time I was eight, I'd outgrown the corridor but my brother, aged five, still made motor bicycle noises as he raced his tricycle up and down and reversed it at speed in the doorway of the broom cupboard. Then he zoomed off again up to the nursery end, circumnavigating the round table where I was painting. This manoeuvre, though skilled, caused the table to jiggle and my paint water to spill. At such times these two little birds did not agree.

When the sun came out on what should have been an all-wet afternoon, I felt cheated. At that late hour, going out meant nothing more than a short walk on damp pavements, for there was no time to get to the park or our local 'green lung' the Chelsea Pensioners' Gardens. I walked gloomily wearing my raincoat 'just in case', avoided the pavement joins, and wished I was indoors again.

I have grown to like really wet walks, that is when I am dressed for the weather in an encompassing plastic raincoat, my old for-and-aft fisherman's hat on my head and gummers on my feet. At first I try to stay as dry as I can but there comes a moment when one is wet enough to abandon the struggle and a fine sense of recklessness takes over. Then it's good to stride out across fields of knee-high soaking grass and deliberately choose to splodge through mud at gateways and deep into puddles in the lanes. The getting home again is nice, too; a slight, unreasonable feeling of virtue accompanied by relief that it is over, also the knowledge that, morally, there is no need to go out again that day rounds off the glow.

Rain can add light to the city scene – street lamps reflected, rain drops lit up along railings. Outside my window in London is a beautiful plane tree, an elegant skeleton in winter, an embroidery of tender greens in spring, a thick canopy in summer. I like it most in winter when the heavy leftover seedpods, like a fat bobble fringe on a Victorian tablecloth, toss in the wet wind; and rain on the bare bones of the tree illuminates it with a sleek wet sea-lion look. Rains come our way from the West and I see an Impressionist painting as I lie in bed watching the elegant black branches blurred through my rain pocked window.

We get plenty of rain in England; or so you might think. Yet when there is a dry spell for longer than three weeks someone is sure to start talking of droughts. But I have also been in Africa when the rains are supposed to arrive and don't. Clouds may pile up but they are an empty mockery and don't dampen. In the bush you can smell the rain coming and it is a fragrant moment when the skies have blackened and trees lash about in the rising wind and that unmistakable waft of rain scents the air as it moves across dry lands. Then the children run out, arms outstretched, mouths open to catch the huge drops; and there is rejoicing.

When I was a child I wanted freckles (one day I even painted them on my nose). Walking in the rain once I suddenly discovered that rain on the face gave me the feeling I had freckles, and I have never lost this small pleasure. Even now, I still like lifting up my face to the rain and feeling freckled. ■

This article first appeared in the Christian Science Monitor in 1974.

JOYCE'S FAMILY AND FRIENDS

Joyce aged 5 and her
2-year-old brother Tommy, 1915

'My Father'

My father taught me that discipline is not so much as thou-shalt-*not* as it is way through to thou *canst.* Music and dance students accepted this without question; but drama and creative writing students felt they must express themselves and that too much self-discipline might block their imaginative impulses. The dancers and musicians pointed out that until you mastered your instrument through the sheer discipline of practising, you couldn't express anything very clearly.

Joyce with her mother, Nora, and brother Tommy in about 1925

PARRS, CLIVEDEN, TAPLOW, BUCKS. BURNHAM 460.

I did my hair a new way that night I'll see if I can draw it.

The black velvet bow is essential because it is the only way I can secure the uplifted side bits

This is a last year's dress. but refreshed with black vel. bows on the black vel. bodice. The skirt is pale blue tafeta.

Joyce and her mother Nora were very close. Here is a letter from Joyce to Nora from 1938

Virginia

The writer Virginia Graham and Joyce first met when they were seven years old. Both Christian Scientists, they remained best friends for the next sixty years. They wrote to each other every day when they were apart, sometimes even on days when they had already met. Before Joyce flew with Reggie to South Africa in 1975 she posted this to Virginia.

Darling Ginnie

Every time I left England during the war and afterwards for the US, Canada and the long Australian trips, I always wrote you a farewell letter and left it in the bank to be delivered in the event of my departure for other realms. Time and again I tore them up. This time I'm writing, not via the bank, but direct to my Best Friend simply to record the fact of my gratitude and appreciation for ALL she does for me day in and day out, with imagination, selflessness and just straight loving-kindness.

If I appear to take it for granted this letter is to assure you I DON'T. I'm AMAZED and moved and delighted by all the good that comes my way through you, darling, and TA for it ALL.

How rich we are to have this kind of long-lasting friendship and affection. What a marvellous thing it is and what a cause for re-joicing and thanking-God-for.

At this moment, 1.30 p.m. we are packed but not yet into our tropical wear. It really is a stinker, innit. Rain in rods.

Love and thoughts and certainly about you and your Life and well being. Mine too - and all of us - thank God.

Love Joyce.

Virginia wrote this about Joyce soon after she died.

Joyce's total enjoyment of life was the keynote to her character. She had a genuine love of goodness and sought it in all things, in music, literature, nature and, above all, people. Her talent was unique in that although she caricatured her subjects and pinpointed their idiosyncrasies, there was never a hint of censure. She seemed to be doing it all for fun; and her manifest zest for living coupled with her artistry, kind-heartedness, and sense of humour had a cherishing effect on her audiences.

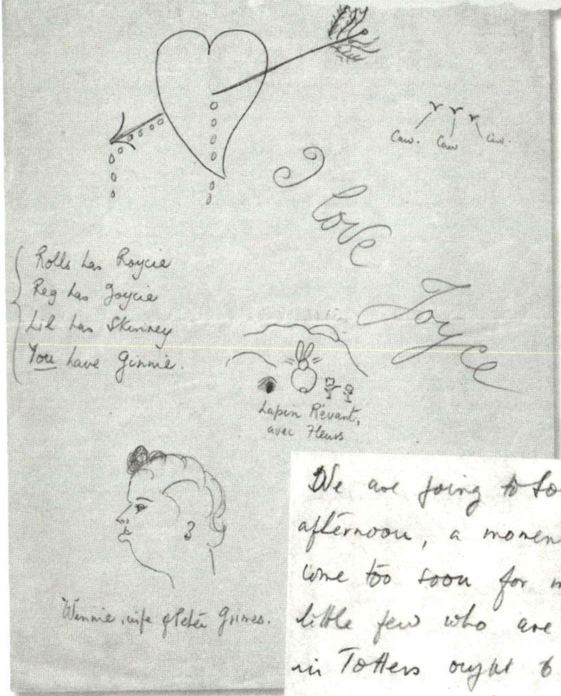

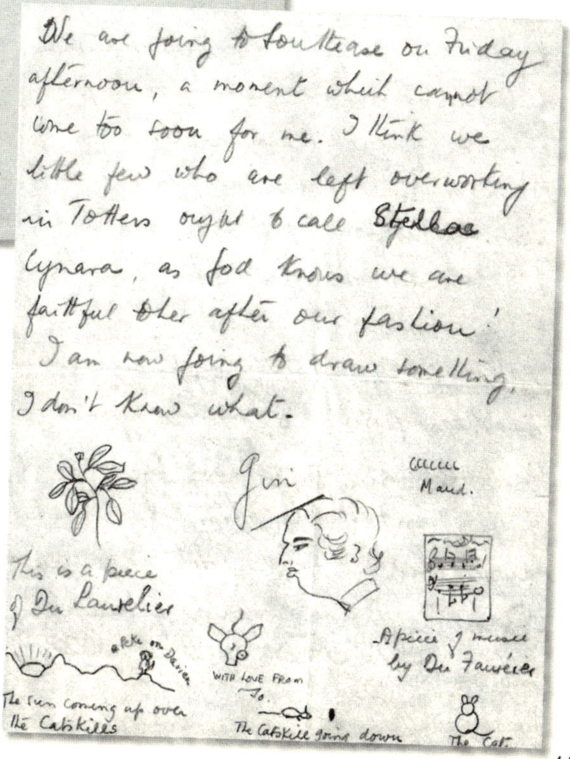

We are going to Southease on Friday afternoon, a moment which cannot come too soon for me. I think we little few who are left overworking in Totters ought to call [illegible] Cynara, as God knows we are faithful Other after our fashion!
I am now going to draw something, I don't know what.

This is a piece of Du Lauvelier

Gin

Maud.

A piece of music by Du Fauvelier

Pike on Darien

WITH LOVE FROM Jo.

The sun coming up over the Catskills

The Catskill going down

The Cat.

Letter from Virginia

Verily

Joyce was nominated president of the Society of Women Writers and Journalists in 1957. Another member was her friend, the writer Verily Anderson, whose family called the society 'The Wild Women'. In 1976 Verily was unable to attend the annual general meeting, so Joyce wrote to tell her about it. Anyone who has ever chaired a long-winded speaker will recognise Joyce's quandary with Paul Scott, author of *The Raj Quartet*. This letter demonstrates how her theatre and radio experience made her expect the highest standards from everyone.

At the hairdressers for a Perm
30 May 1976

My Darling Verily

You were much missed at the SWWJ on Weds. A mammoth day all rather compressed because Stationer's Hall was to be occupied by the Queen Mum at 7 and we had to be out by 5. Our speaker was Paul Scott, novelist not known to me but I have an elderly aunt who much enjoys his books about life in India. He seemed a pleasant study type in mid-50s, with rather a powerful beery aroma about him but no sign of wobble. So it wasn't that that caused him to over-run so largely. Before we began I explained that the tightness of our schedule made it vital to finish his talk at 3.15. Easy, he said, it will take much less that that. We began 5 minutes early. It was a good & fascinating talk about the British Raj called 'Sahibs & Mem Sahibs' and he has an ironic manner and a dry humour. I feared he was going to take the easy way & mock the Britons who worked in India but no. After an initial setting of the scene he revealed admiration for the fresh-faced young Englishmen who ruled over areas as big as Denmark with devotion and humour. At 3.10 I could see he still had at least 20 more pages to go. (His script was alarmingly fat, between hard covers.) How to remind him that 3.15 was coming up? I had put my little folding clock on the table between us. I touched it lightly, casually - as if I was merely playing with it! He took no notice. Three minutes later in response to looks from the Chairman, from the committee, and observing nodders-off in front rows, I laid flat the little clock, face up. He looked down. 'What time is it?' I told him. 'Oh', he said. Pause. Air tense with apprehension. . . I wondered if it was possible to summarise. . .? No, he said. But he found a letter he had incorporated in his script written by Somerset Maugham & read it as a sort of summing up. And at 3.20 we clapped him vociferously; he deserved it for an excellent, fascinating talk - too slowly spoken and without a look at the time. He said, hurt I fear, that he had never over-run, ever, as if it was my fault. Some members thought I should not have stopped him, what did it matter if we had tea later? But that wasn't as simple as it seemed. Tea had to be brought in, served, cleared and country-members wanted to meet friends before they caught trains etc etc; also there was a consensus who wanted it to be over. Stopping him was one of the most agonising things I've ever had to do. He didn't like it one bit, either! I did my very best to smooth his ruffled feathers & assure him, with truth, that it was a good & gripping talk. We had tea together and I think he went away somewhat comforted. But, dammit, it was his own fault. Talkers must keep their eyes on the time. He swore he had taped his piece the day before and it had under-run. I know only too well that a programme carefully timed at home to run for an hour can easily spread to an hour and a quarter when it is performed to an audience.

When I'm doing talks (currently titled 'What can happen to a housewife when she isn't looking') I have yet to get it all in in the time span and, so far, I haven't once been able to include all I've prepared. But I've ever been time-conscious and being an improviser I can & do bring it to a stop well-within the given space. So I feel that Paul Scott only had himself to blame. Anyway it was a horrid experience for your president! I wrote him a letter of thanks, praise & apology; I also rang him up so I hope & trust his ego is itself again - whew. . . . It was a good talk; could have been much better if pruned and less self-indulgently delivered.

It was a good meeting. Business like with an accent on professionalism. I quoted Shirley's Girlfriend speaking of professional musicians - 'I mean he can do it even when he isn't in the mood' and I think that's not a bad definition of what professional means, do you?

I've gone on far too long,

lots of love to you from us both Joyce

'An Ideal Husband'

Joyce's closest friend was her husband Reggie. They were married in 1929, when Joyce was only nineteen and Reggie Pascoe Grenfell, a trainee accountant, was twenty-six. Joyce wrote this article for The News Chronicle in 1952, after 23 years with Reggie. They remained happily married until Joyce's death fifty years later.

OF COURSE there isn't such a thing as a universally approved Ideal Husband and thank goodness for that, and anyway Ideal for whom?

If you are a woman who can't read, cook, sew or sit quiet, you aren't going to want a husband who prefers to spend his leisure at home. Your ideal husband is probably what is known as a 'sport'; a taker-outer; rich, glossy and gay.

On the other hand if your passion in life is hiking and playing the recorder it's no good marrying a man who doesn't like walking or wood-wind.

Neither of these last two gentlemen would appeal to me, but it takes all sorts to make a world and love is a wonderful thing.

There is only one essential in all ideal husbands. They must believe they have chosen well. After all, it is fairly important to like each other. A simple thing, but it lies at the heart of the whole business.

There are no rules about the looks of an ideal husband. Love *is* blind. You set out at 17 knowing with steady certainty that the ideal must have fair hair, stand six feet six in his socks, have long sensitive fingers and a baritone voice, and you end up with a square-shaped husband, five feet seven with blunt hands and red hair who can't carry a tune in a basket.

Or perhaps you know, deep down in the heart of you, that the man for you has got to be athletic and jolly handy with a tool box and intelligent about horses and you find happiness with a left-wing intellectual whose lack of humour matches your own and who knows all about Kafka and very little else.

There is some truth, I expect, in the attraction of opposites, and it is a good thing to have different tastes for your outside interests, but you must see eye to eye about essentials like warmth, humour and the meaning of values.

Reliability has come to imply dullness, but it is an important quality in an ideal husband and one I would demand in mine. It doesn't just mean remembering to call at the butchers on the way home or being a creature of habit. It means having a sense of responsibility and that means having a certain selflessness.

The dullest couples, anyway to the outside world, are those in which all interest is centred on one partner. It may make a wife happy to be slave, doormat and handmaiden, but the balance is wrong and if anything should happen to one of them the other is lost. Undivided attention is an unfair weight to load on to anyone, man, woman, or child. It is another form of self-indulgence I think and deserves what it gets, but it's always sad when it does.

Ideally, a married couple should be made of two complete individuals who shine the most brightly for being together. It is the most important thing in the world – I say this solemnly – to be of first concern to someone, but this relationship is a delicate thing, and only by individual completeness can it be maintained.

Kay Hammond told us in a recent *We Beg To Differ* radio programme about the cynic who said at the wedding: 'They're sure to be happy, they're both so in love with him.' My bet is that misery sets in quite early on. But you never know, the Ideal Husband to some women is a helpless, childlike, creature needing constant attention. Ideal to some, but not to me.

With all his integrity and reliability I would like an element of surprise in my Ideal Husband.

'You-never-know-where-you-are-with-him' may keep some girls on their toes but I'd rather be in on the secret. On the other hand fresh discoveries of a pleasing nature are delightful as the years go by.

I like the type of man who talks so attractively and well that he makes me feel actually intelligent and who pays me the compliment of appearing to listen *and* to be interested in what I say.

I must be able to respect my I.H. too. It is nice, of course, if he can read and write and do sums and it is a definite advantage if he is clean, can cook and is generally good about the house. I am in favour of solvency, an equable temperament, enthusiasm and an interest in life.

I would like him to play tennis just well enough, to wear white shirts, be liked by my friends and be a great deal cleverer than I am. I think intuition is enough for a wife, but it is just as well if one of the pair has a brain. My I.H. would not be a politician in any party and he would never be at home for lunch except at weekends.

If only I could introduce you to my husband, then I wouldn't have to explain, as we are nicely suited.

Joyce and Reggie together in about 1935

Shirley's Girl Friend

Although Shirley's girlfriend was fictional, she was with Joyce for so long that she was almost part of the family. After the Second World War Joyce wrote and performed a BBC radio series called A Note with Music. One of the programme's stars was an unnamed Cockney girl whom Joyce called 'Shirley's Girlfriend'. She had a boyfriend called Norm 'the one who drives a lorry with big ears'. Shirl's friend later appeared on the West End stage, with her face powder by 'Dawn O'May – Chiffon Mist Facial Gauze'. Here she is in 'Wedge Heels' from the radio of 1947.

Shirley - Shirl, do stop knitting and look at me new shoes. Wedge heels - the latest one and a 'arf inch platform soles. The girl in the shop said they added a dignity to me, but I keep fallin' off 'em. Well, I'm not used to being up so high. See? I'll get used to 'em in time, and they say you can dance lovely in them - if you don't fall down.

No, I didn't want them really - not wedge heels. I was looking for a more everyday sort of shoe, really, but the girl says no-one's wearin' shoes with just heels now, and you want to be in the fashion, she says, don't you?' And I says, 'Well I don't know.' And she said, '*Well*, if Madam is satisfied bein' old fashioned far be it for me to urge Madam to purchase somethin' Madam doesn't fancy.' And she started to put away these shoes and give me a pityin' sort of look.

'Well,' I says, 'have you got a pair in navy or black like?' I was thinkin' of me floral silk coat. And she says, 'O no-one's wearin' navy or black this season. You want Chelsea Pensioner Red or Giddy Green.' And I says 'Do I?'

And she says, 'Yes, they're straight from the Continent, them colours, and the models is trimmed with art crocodile and the platform soles is studded with big brass nails.'

'Oo,' I says, 'they'd see me comin', wouldn't they?'

And she says, 'If Madam does not fancy bein' looked at, Madam isn't obliged to buy here,' and she started to pick bits of invisible dust off 'er dress with 'er eyebrows all raised up to show she didn't think much of me. She made me feel awful, Shirl, I wanted to get up and walk out past her, but me legs wouldn't carry me.

So I says, 'Have you got them in honey?' And she says 'No-one's wearin' honey this season', and gives a little yawn like, and looks at her watch. And then she says, 'What size are you?' and I tell her and she says, 'O, you are an awkward size, aren't you. But I think I could find you a pair in Paradise Purple but not in Chelsea Pensioner or Giddy Green.' And she goes off to have a look. O, I did want to get up and go, but I couldn't, I was stuck to me seat.

Back she come and I slip me old shoes off and try to hide them under me chair - I got me best semi-fully-fashioned on so I didn't mind 'er havin' a look at me feet, and of course the shoes fitted. Well, she said they did, and I expect they will when I've eased 'em in a bit. Bit noisy, aren't they? Paradise Purple. They may tone down a bit when I get 'em wet. Norm hasn't seen them yet. But he will, he will.

JOYCE OUT AND ABOUT

'Ambling'

Joyce lived in Chelsea for most of her life, but it was only when she had unexpected spare time that she could really explore it properly. She wrote about this exploration in the Christian Science Monitor in 1973.

WHAT do you do with an unexpected gift of unplanned time? We found ourselves with a beautifully empty engagement book where we had thought to find it full and spilling over. Of course we didn't go to the galleries and concerts we'd always said we would go to if only we had the time; nor did we read the whole of Tolstoy. One of the things we did do, though, was to amble and discover, slowly and on foot, the back streets of our London 'village'.

Like New York, London is made up of hundreds of small 'villages' where the locals shop, and post mail, and get the dry cleaning done. In our 'London village' of Fulham Road, you can get most of the daily necessities and extra luxuries at our delicatessen. You can no longer get a spool of thread, or a button. Do fewer people need buttons and thread? They get harder to track down, although the next village of King's Road still sells these things in a few basic but undistinguishable colours.

What I didn't know at all well, until our unplanned ambling time, were the small side streets behind the main road. Here you find early 19th century houses with little gardens front and back, window boxes and sometimes even a tree. All have flowers somewhere.

The month that was unexpectedly bestowed on us was in summer, when the gardens were exuberant. One Regency house, freshly painted dazzling white, appeared to be rising out of a ruffled petticoat of petunias, planted in tubs close together. White flowers were set off by striped red, pinks, purple and mauves – it was a veritable explosion.

In the ordinary way I am always en route somewhere, with a fixed time of arrival at the end of the journey, so I take the main roads. Ambling means you don't have to be anywhere particularly at any special time, so I pause to look at gardens and grapevines – yes, grapevines – in London. They grow well here and climb up drainpipes to the tiny wrought iron balconies that are too delicate to step out onto but nevertheless qualify as balconies.

I also pause to speak to an occasional cat.

I must declare that I am not a cat woman, there is no natural bond between us. Among other things, I don't like being sprung up on even though I can admire the leap. But a cat met on an amble tends to stay on the ground and rub against what it assumes must be a friendly leg.

Midmorning is a good time for encountering cats in a relaxed mood. Pre-school children are to be seen riding their tricycles up and down small paths in tiny front gardens. Sometimes they come to the front gate and tell you the names of some of their brothers and sisters. And of their cat. They tell you what they did yesterday. And now that they've got a captive audience, would we like to see them ride their tricycles? Child-watching is a ploy I like, so I say Yes.

Once when we were in Australia, we met a three-year-old called Simon who had just mastered the art of hopping. It is a great moment when you find you can travel on one leg, and Simon was aflame with the success of it. We are contemporaries of his grandparents, with whom we were staying. So you will understand how pleased I was when Simon fell in love with me. There was one slight flaw: he believed I was my husband's mother.

After breakfast he would say to my husband, 'Shall we go and see your mother?' and together they visited me in my room where I was writing letters.

'Hullo,' said Simon, already standing on one foot. 'Would you like to see me hop?'

'Oh *yes*,' I said encouragingly. With infinite concentration and heavy breathing he jerked his way across the room, fair hair bouncing on his forehead, his face growing rose with the effort.

'Well done,' I said, ready to get back to my letter writing.

'Would you like to see me hop again?'

'Well - yes, of course.'

It could have turned into perpetual motion but to be frank, you do get to the end of hopping fairly soon when you are only the watcher.

The speed of life at midmorning in the shaded side streets of our London 'village' is delightfully *lento*. You seldom see anyone hurrying. Housewives can be seen moving about in upstairs rooms. Some are already in the garden-level kitchen starting to prepare the midday meal. Babies, put out into their perambulators to sleep, don't always nod off at once and you can hear them talking in gurgles. You can also hear music from a piano somewhere. Retired citizens are out ambling as we are, and there is time to smile and mention the weather and the garden we are admiring. Time, as W.H. Davies wrote, 'To stand and stare'.

Back in the 'village' the pace quickens - we stand in line to buy zucchini and peaches.

'Life keeping you busy these days?' enquires Arthur at the fruiterers.

'No, I'm just ambling.'

'Lovely,' he says.

I agree.

Suppressed Conversations

The following extracts of conversations were written by Joyce for Everywoman magazine in 1951, but we have all heard them when we go out and about. And somehow we know exactly what the speakers sound and look like.

At a cocktail party
. . . the moment I saw you. I said there is a man with the sort of face one can talk to about anything. One knows instantly. At least I do. I mean I *knew* you were the sort of person one could say to quite suddenly, 'Look, I'm madly hungry, let's go in search of a kipper – somewhere – anywhere,' and you'd understand. I'm afraid I'm hopelessly unconventional, I mean life is so boring unless one has fun. My family think I'm quite mad, but I believe you are too . . .

In the Post Office
. . . I want it to get there by the Thursday, you see, because it is for my nephew's birthday. He's twenty-two this year. He had his twenty-first *last* year. We all think the world of Alan. His name is Alan. I'm sending him a pullover; nothing very extra but he's fussy. Won't wear shop woollies. No, it has to be like auntie does! So it must get there by Thursday, you see . . .

At the Stationer's
. . . a card for a four-year old girl. It's my little god-daughter and she tells everyone 'I'se fwee now but I'se four next.' Oh, she is a comic. You can't help making a fuss of her. She's got this naturally curly hair, more of a gold colour, and these huge eyes. Blue. You wouldn't have a card with 'For Wendy' on it? Never mind, as long as it says four it will be all right. She knows what a 4 looks like, you see, and I've told her Win, that's me, I've told her Win'd be sending her a nice card so she'll be expecting it. And I've got her a little plastic bag so she can go shopping just like Mummy! Oh. She is a comic . . .

In the Arts and Crafts Shop

. . . a wee pottery bunny for the mantelpiece. Orange please, because that is my friend's lucky colour. She's a Leo, you see. She's got quite a little collection and they're all named. The ivory elephant is called Ada and the two china dogs are Beaumont and Fletcher and she's got a heavenly duck called the Quack Doctor! I thought it was high time a bunny joined the throng and I fell for that little orange one. I shall tell her it's called Primrose because we've been discussing Disraeli . . .

In the Bus

. . . so late, this would be a crawler. My friend's train gets in at ten to and she's a foreigner; from Sweden. She is over here to study. Well, a friend of mine – my sister-in-law, as a matter of fact – only she is my friend too, because I knew her before she married my brother. Well, she, my sister-in-law that is, got to know her at the International Club she belongs to, and she asked me if I'd take this Swedish girl and show her London one afternoon, so I said I would, but I don't know what she'll do if she gets to the station and I'm not there. She's a got a beautiful singing voice, they all say . . .

At the Hairdresser's

. . . terribly intuitive. I don't think I'm any more psychic than anyone else, but it's just that I feel things more deeply, I suppose, I mean I literally starve without beauty, don't you, Miss Dulcie . . .

In a Tea-Shop
. . . can't help noticing your lapel brooch. My daughter has one very similar only hers is a Mexican sombrero with a pair of little boots dangling from it, she had it sent from abroad, they are so unusual, aren't they? She likes anything unusual, and of course her flat is beautifully fitted up. She's done her lounge up like an Old English Inn and has the TV hidden in an old grandfather clock case. Her husband is in the electrical trade so they've got *everything*, electric kettle, and cooker – and a blanket . . .

On a Bench in the Park
. . . down Tatters. I'm so sorry. He's a bit friendly, I'm afraid, aren't you, old boy? Quiet, Tatters, good dog. Down. I said *down*. We're a bit over-excited, aren't we, Tatters? We're velly velly excited that's what we are because Daddy is coming home tomorrow. Gently, gently, mind my coat. Yes, my husband is coming back tomorrow after a year at sea . . .

Outside the Theatre
. . . the symbolism of the cockney maid was engaging. And when he realised the truth at last, the way he just stood there and suffered. He really felt it. He can't have been acting. His face was too blank. And full of suffering. There was a sense of tragedy about his whole being. Even his feet were tragic, so it can't have been acting. Nobody can act tragic feet . . .

Favourite London Characters

These Favourite London characters were described by Joyce in three talks called 'Bus conductors', 'London Eccentrics', and 'Elderly Friends' broadcast on the BBC North American Service in 1957.

The rag and bone man gets all over London. I've seen him in widely different districts pushing his little handcart loaded down with old iron bedsteads, cooking pots, jam jars and sacks full of mysterious objects. He always wears a battered top hat and around it, like candles round a cake, stand a row of pigeon feathers, I suppose collected from Trafalgar Square. This little man sings loudly to himself as he pushes his barrow in among the traffic. Bus drivers and taxi men call out to him in a good natured bantering way but he just winks back and goes on singing.

Another familiar eccentric wears thick soled ski-ing boots in every weather and a blue trapper's cap with furry ear flaps. In summer these are tied on top. He is always shopping when I see him, carrying a shiny black oil cloth bag and leading his drop-tailed dog. I think he probably dreams of northern climes and dresses to go with the dreams. But his dog is a bit of a let-down. He hasn't got a vestige of Husky or Samoyard about him, just a dim little white-ish terrier with the dash gone out of him.

And then there is the Pekinese Woman. She is elderly and large and she has seven or eight Peke dogs. Some of them are very very old and these she wheels in a basket on roller skates, three at a time. The others wuffle behind her, trailing their feathers and stopping as Pekes do just to be difficult and get their own way. I think the Pekinese woman centres her whole life around these dogs and when I see her out with them it is part of an elaborate dogs' day programme. They are well groomed and fed, and so is she, except for her hat. This is knitted, and must have once kept a teapot warm. Down the street goes this little procession, back to a stuffy little flat somewhere. I imagine it with a lot of Chinese bric-à-brac and special dog chairs and dog mats and rows of dog drinking bowls. I think they all have names like Wang and Ping and Tai-ho. You can see that they are all happy, including the Pekinese Woman.

I have several friends among the conductors on the bus route near my home. One is a very cheerful young man who never wears a hat. He is always good-humoured and sings as he lurches along the decks collecting fares. He is good at making you feel welcome aboard his bus. Even in rush hours, he takes trouble over the passengers and is kind to the elderly ones who need a hand getting off. One day I was on my way to do a matinée in the West End and we had a long philosophical talk about his work. All of a sudden he unbuttoned his jacket and took out an old and pretty silver watch that he kept in a little chamois leather bag. 'See this,' he said, 'this was left to me by a passenger. He was a nice old gent, used to ride with me up to his club every day and we'd talk and laugh and I used to look out for him. Then he went and died and he left me his watch. He didn't know my name but he put in his will that it was for "the cheerful young conductor on the number 22 bus that never wears a hat". Well the Transport Board enquired at my depot and found it was me.' He looked at the watch and said, 'He was a very nice gent, he was.'

Another bus conductor friend goes by the patriotic name of Mr Britain. He is a handsome man, no longer very young, with a very erect military bearing. It seems he heard me on the radio and recognised me the first time not by my face, but by my voice. He lives in the East End and every Christmas he gets up a party for the children down there. He is most courteous and would never embarrass me by referring to my work. I used to live opposite a bus stop and Mr Britain knew this so he wrote a very polite letter asking me if I could come to his Christmas party, and sing a song 'or something'. So down I went and there was Mr Britain conducting his party with just as much talent as he conducts his bus. I sang, he sang, and we all sang together and when I left he gave me an enormous box of chocolates tied with a pink bow.

One of my London friends is the stage door keeper of St Martin's Theatre where I have often played. Joe is 83 years old and has *some* teeth but they live in a little box at home, because Joe likes it better that way. Until a few months ago he had one prized natural tooth - the last of the lot and a good stayer - he told me, for he'd had it, solo, for *many* years. Then he bit into a pear, of all innocent things, and that was the end of that. Joe's complaint is that now he can't keep his pipe steady without that tooth, drat it.

Joe lives with his mother-in-law, known as 'The Old Lady', for she is 96, and Joe's son, 'The Boy' who is a mere 30 or so. Joe married late and lost his wife all too soon but he has a happy home with these two.

He was a clown once and played in Paris, he went to Russia with his dancing act and toured the music halls all over this country as both artist and manager. He can still sing and dance and will do so with the slightest encouragement. He has a direct and refreshing approach that blows away a lot of cobwebs where they need blowing.

JOYCE ON MUSIC

Joyce's Favourite Music

Joyce felt that music was 'a bond, a language, even if you don't know all the grammar'. She never studied it formally, but listened to the radio and went to so many concerts that she was on the panel of the television series *Face the Music*. She was one of the very few people to appear twice on the BBC radio programme *Desert Island Discs*: in 1951 and in 1971. Her choice of luxury item was writing and drawing material, and her book in addition to *The Bible* and the *Complete Works* of Shakespeare was Mary Baker Eddy's *Science and Health, with Key to the Scriptures*.

Jimmy Edwards, Stanley Holloway, Gracie Fields and Cicely Courtneidge also appeared in 1951. In the summer of 1971, Geoffrey Boycott, Jonathan Miller, Billie Whitelaw and John Braine also participated.

Desert Island Discs

Bach, Toccata in G, played by her friend the pianist Myra Hess.
Dvorak, Cello Concerto in D minor (opus 104), played by Pablo Cassalls.
Rachmaninov, Vocalise (opus 34, no 14) played by the Boston Symphony Orchestra conducted by Koussevitsky.
The Trolley Song from the film *Meet me in St Louis*, sung by Judy Garland, composed by Joyce's friend Hugh Martin.
Enrique Granados, 'El Mirar de la maja' from *Tonadillas* sung by Victoria de los Angeles with Gerald Moore at the piano.
Bach, Ricercare a 6 voci, from *The Musical Offering*, played by the Kammerorchester and Edwin Fischer.
Oskar Strauss, 'Depuis trois ans passés' from *Mariette* sung by Yvonne Printemps.
Henry Purcell, 'Nymphs & Shepherds', sung by Manchester schoolchildren, played by the Hallé Orchestra.

Joyce's choice on her second visit to the Desert Island in 1971 included three pieces by Bach, two by Mozart, and featured her friends Myra Hess, Benjamin Britten and the Irish singer Mary O'Hara.

Victoria Campbell Graham Payn Joyce Grenfell

are introduced by Noël Coward in
WORDS AND MUSIC
at 9.35

'On Music'

Joyce wrote this article for the magazine Everywoman in 1952.

Do you like music? Good.

The world, it seems is divided into those who love, listen to, hear and understand music; those who say they love music and never really listen; and those who have the courage to admit they don't know or mind what they are missing.

It is the middle groups that fills the big concert halls.

My musical history began when I was sick from on overdose of 'This is the way the farmer goes – clipperty, clop', with practical illustrations. My mother plays the guitar and by the time I was three we sang in parts. I held the tune.

Soon after this, in the First World War, I caught a song called 'The Tattooed Lady' from an American airman and was immediately forbidden to sing it. However, I never forgot it and it served me well in the Second World War. It is an inoffensive little lyric and has these two immortal lines that have long puzzled me: 'And right near her kidney, Was a bird's eye view of Sydney.'

Sydney? The city with the bridge in far-off Australia? Or some unknown love? I like to think it is the latter.

It is nearly as rare for anyone to admit that they are not musical as it is to admit they have no sense of humour. An elderly man I know took a sea voyage many years ago, and when they called at Cape Town a famous actor joined the ship. The local band came down to the quay to play him away, and my friend was noticed by his wife standing at attention, his hat loyally removed from his head. The tune was not the National Anthem, as he supposed, but 'Auld Lang Syne'.

It is interesting to note how people who say they love music behave when classical music comes over the air. 'Heavenly', they murmur, as they close their eyes to indicate sensitivity; then as they lose the thread of the 'tune' they whisper how *witty* Mozart is. Soon the whispering hardens into talk and in no time they are off on more interesting subjects such as food or a really reliable hand cream.

I once heard an otherwise quite balanced woman say she thought Bach was like nothing but five-finger exercises, she preferred Mozart, 'Just like the china ornaments on the mantelpiece.' I counted up to ten before I spoke, and then it was of other things.

Just what leads one to the piano-accordion or the cornet is a secret kept from me. But I suppose there is great satisfaction in overpowering a double bass. All I've ever dreamed about getting into personal contact with are the piano and the human voice. I've sung all my life in an unimportant way. An anonymous postcard sent care of the BBC flooded me with gloom by simply asking in one sinister line: 'Who told you you could sing?'

One of my favourite pastimes is watching choral societies at work. There is something fascinating about those ladies and gentlemen launched on their own sea of sound. When they are good one never notices what they look like, but when they aren't very...

I once helped with a small choir. We formed it in our Women's Institute and we sang with vigour. After a while it was decided that we should go in for a local music festival, so we sent for the set song.

My pleasure in choirs rose as I watched our widely assorted shapes and sizes singing with deep intensity 'The Wild Brown Bee Is my Lover'. Alas, we did no good in the competition and soon after this I left the village.

I am told that listening to people singing in close harmony is painful to real musicians. In America no picnic is complete without everyone harmonizing sooner or later. Preferably later, under a large moon.

Some people like brass bands – so do I, on occasions. Some people like only Light music, whatever that is, or Wagner. Without sounding pompous I would like to say that I like *all* music – but it must be good of its kind: swing, chamber, opera, choral, dance, symphonic, and even musical comedy.

National Gallery Concerts

At the start of the Second World War, Joyce helped make sandwiches for the famous lunchtime concerts at London's National Gallery in Trafalgar Square. On 1 January 1940 Kenneth Clark, not a musician but the director of the gallery, conducted Haydn's Toy Symphony with an array of famous musicians. The pianist Myra Hess and singer Irene Scharrer played the 'cuckoo'; pianist Benno Moisewitsch was on triangle; Elena Gerhardt on toy drums and pianist Clifford Curzon banged the cymbal. Joyce was invited to play the nightingale – an exacting part of six bars on the water whistle. The next day she wrote this poem.

National Gallery, New Years Day, 1940

Dear Haydn, Where 'ere you be
Did you on the First of Jan
Hear your own Toy Symphony
Making glad the heart of man?

Kenneth Clark

Oh it was a sound to hear!
Oh it was a sight to see
Full twelve hundred crowding near
At the National Galleree.
Maestro Clark took up his stand;
All, at once, was tense and still.
When he raised a ruling hand
Off we went in style, with skill.
Cuckoos - Mesdames Hess and Scharrer
Thrilled us to the very marrer.
Plaintive, bold and gay were they
(Birds are seldom heard that way
But this fine display of soul
Added to the joyous whole).
Moisewitsch and Diedrich - quails;
Symonds and Grenfell - nightingales.
Gerhardt, Lassimore, Murdoch too
Played the drums like soldiers do.
Jones and Curzon, rattlers nimble

Vied with Howes upon the cymbal.
Oh, the sweetness of the strings!
Oh, the dulcet bird-like song!
Oh, the fearsome brassy rings!
(Trumpeters: Joyce-Smith and Long.)

Dear Haydn, where so 'ere you be
Did you, on the First of Jan,
Hear your own Toy Symphony
Making glad the heart of man?

1940

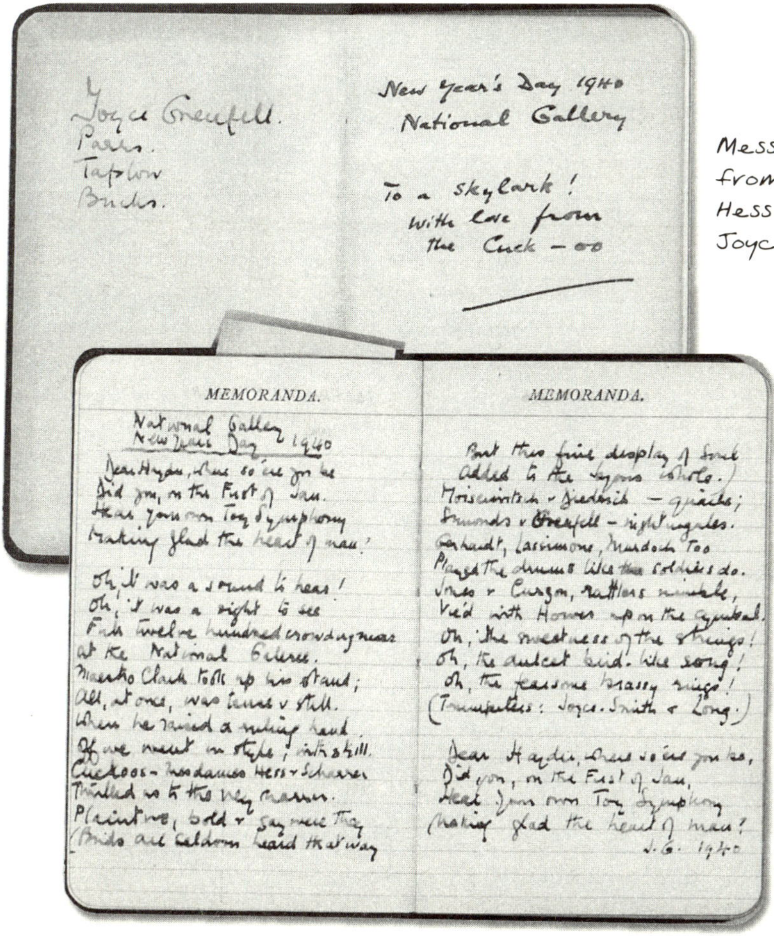

Message from Myra Hess to Joyce

National Gallery poem, 1940

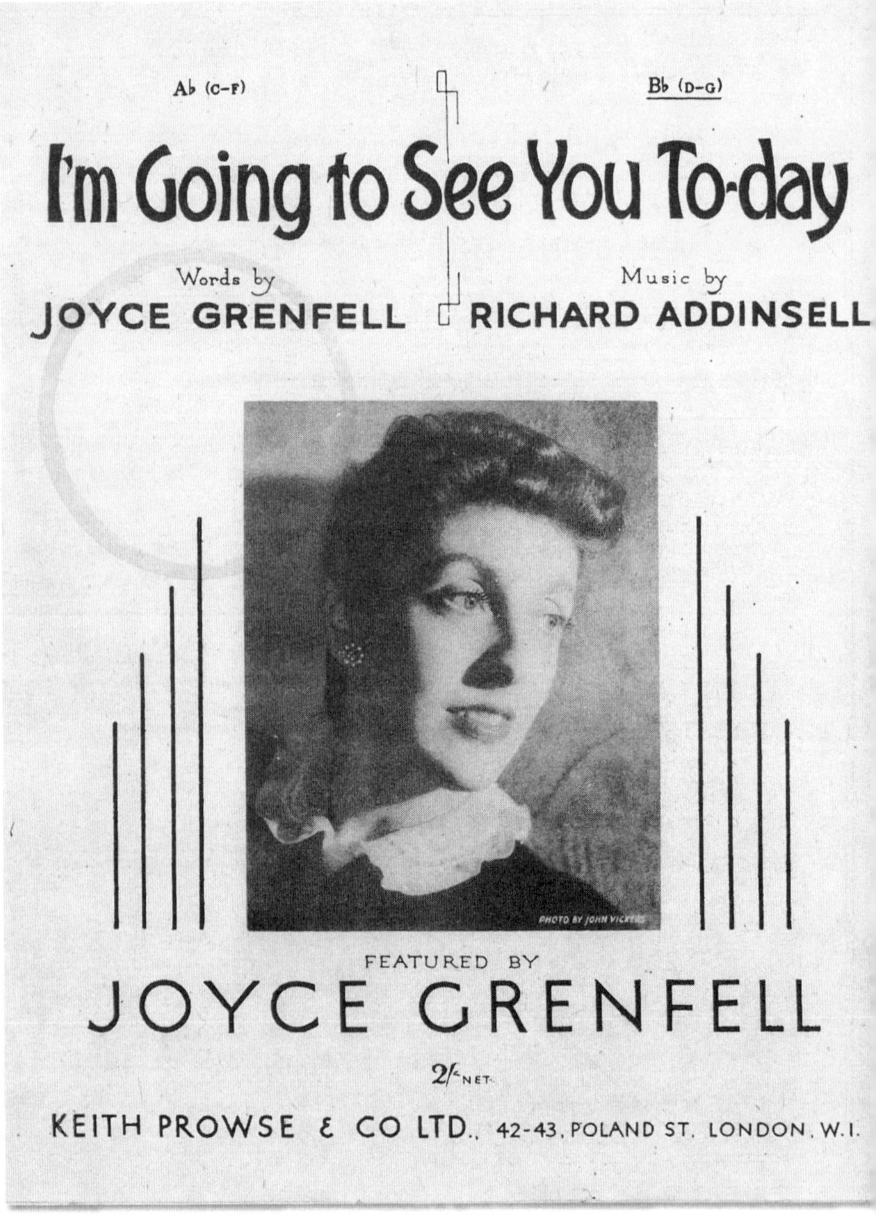
Ab (C–F)
Bb (D–G)
I'm Going to See You To-day
Words by
JOYCE GRENFELL
Music by
RICHARD ADDINSELL
PHOTO BY JOHN VICKERS
FEATURED BY
JOYCE GRENFELL
2/- NET
KEITH PROWSE & CO LTD., 42-43, POLAND ST. LONDON, W.1.

From 1942 Joyce wrote many popular songs with composer Richard Addinsell

CALYPSO

It's the thing to be intellectual
To be Third programme is effectual
It's a hell of a struggle and to win the fight
You've got to be able to read and write.

Yes, you've got to keep up your education.
You can't waste time on recreation.
Have you been reading any good books lately?
Nor have I - it doesn't worry me greatly.

If pursuing the Arts is making you queasy
Come to my house and take it easy,
Intellectuality is all very fine
But maybe you prefer a quiet life like mine?

The Arts Council is backing every kind of culture
Music and Drama and Henry Moore's sculpture
But still a lot of people only start to feel good
On the Wynward side of Mr John Gielgud.

If you've a dizzy headache 'cos you've had a heck of
A Time with Shakespeare and Shaw and Chekov
And though Mary Martin is really terrific
Its warm at my place as the South Pacific.

To sit though an opera the seats are hard on
Unmusical people at Covent Garden,
It's nice to be high-brow but you can feel mouldy
Waiting for Tristan to kiss Isolde.

So come up to my place and leave all the snooty
We can make our own opera as Cosi Fan Tutti
With the kettle singing and the radio blaring
I'll fry you a lovely fresh Albert Herring.

You can wear yourself out if you do much queuin'
For Eileen Joyce or Yehudi Menuhin
But I will play you the works of Fauré
And make the lot con Amore.

So if you've nothing else to do,
I'll be waiting there for you
You don't need to have a key
Just whistle up to me.

I like the intelligentsia, I like the arty
I like to see them at it when I go to a party
But there is one thing I like more
And that's to be behind my own front door.

This was written by Joyce in 1949 and may have originally been set to music - now lost.

JOYCE'S INSPIRATION

The happiest - no, the most fulfilled - people I have met have all one thing in common: an unending sense of discovery and wonder. And enthusiasm. Thank God for zest.

On Happiness

Joyce wrote this radio talk called 'Happiness – can it be pursued' in 1965.

At a recent woman's luncheon I was asked, 'What makes you happy?' I mentioned that one of the most enjoyable times in a woman's day is that glorious moment when she takes off her girdle, roll-on, corset, stays or whatever, and feels the resulting lovely liberty! When I was reported saying this in the world wide press, they got it wrong. For I had *not* been talking about happiness but of much smaller pleasures. Happiness, as I see it, is a far more solid thing and comes from a sense of joy. It is a quiet, strong and deep feeling that may manifest itself as lightness of heart but which is a by-product, the result of a calm sense of 'all's-well'.

I read somewhere that 'Happiness is not having what you want; it is wanting what you have.' This could mean happiness is the resigned settling for, in a grey and defeated way, whatever situation we find ourselves in, without trying to improve it. I think that happiness shines more than that, and is far more nourishing.

Happiness cannot be pursued, it has to be found, recognised, because it is part of everyone's spiritual inheritance. It is a condition free from doubt; and it is always un-self-consciousness. It is complete contentment and that means: contained. We each contain the ingredients for our own fulfilment and wholeness.

Really contented people (not contented like cows, but contained in a place of peace) attract me like a magnet: unspoken joy is contagious. I love that absent-minded undertone singing coming from someone who is simply expressing their contentment. That timeless, gentle sound a woman sometimes makes when she is busy cooking; or a man lets out under his breath while he tinkers. And best of all that spontaneous burbling sound made by very small children lying in their cots discovering shadows and their own toes.

This is not to be confused with 'cheery', the self-congratulatory swoop of soprano or tenor in full aggression. 'I'm always cheerful' is a deadly boast. While I know Pollyanna the Glad Girl is an admirable character, she is more easily acceptable when she doesn't feel compelled to tell us why she is so jolly and glad all the time.

Happiness is the result of sharing, and gratitude, the sense of being part of something eternal and in making discoveries of these things.

Inspiration

I needed some new material for a forthcoming season and my mind was blank. Then I realised that ideas are never scarce; it is only one's panic that blocks the way. With this in mind I stopped fussing and when I next looked back at my year's work, I found I had written more songs and monologues than in any previous year. I now see that ideas are not limited; it is simply a question of being open to them and ready to receive them.

This was a radio talk given by Joyce on Ten to Eight in 1968. She was amazed by the number of listeners of all faiths who wrote to her. She replied to them all.

A SEARCH FOR HUMILITY

It took me years to see why it is necessary - *essential* - to try to get oneself right before one can hope to be of any use to anyone else - or to ones self. I used to think it was wrong to think about oneself - 'just bash on'. Then I saw that to avoid finding out what our true self is, is a kind of opting out - a rootless hope that if you do look closely at yourself and don't like what you see and ignore it, it will go away. But it doesn't . . .

I don't think true humility is a head-down, crawling position, I'd say it was acknowledging the perfect perspective of our true position in the spiritual condition in which we live and move and have our being - the place of confidence; always safe, continuing, good. I think it interesting that in the story of the prodigal son things only began to go right for him when 'he came to himself' - found his true identity.

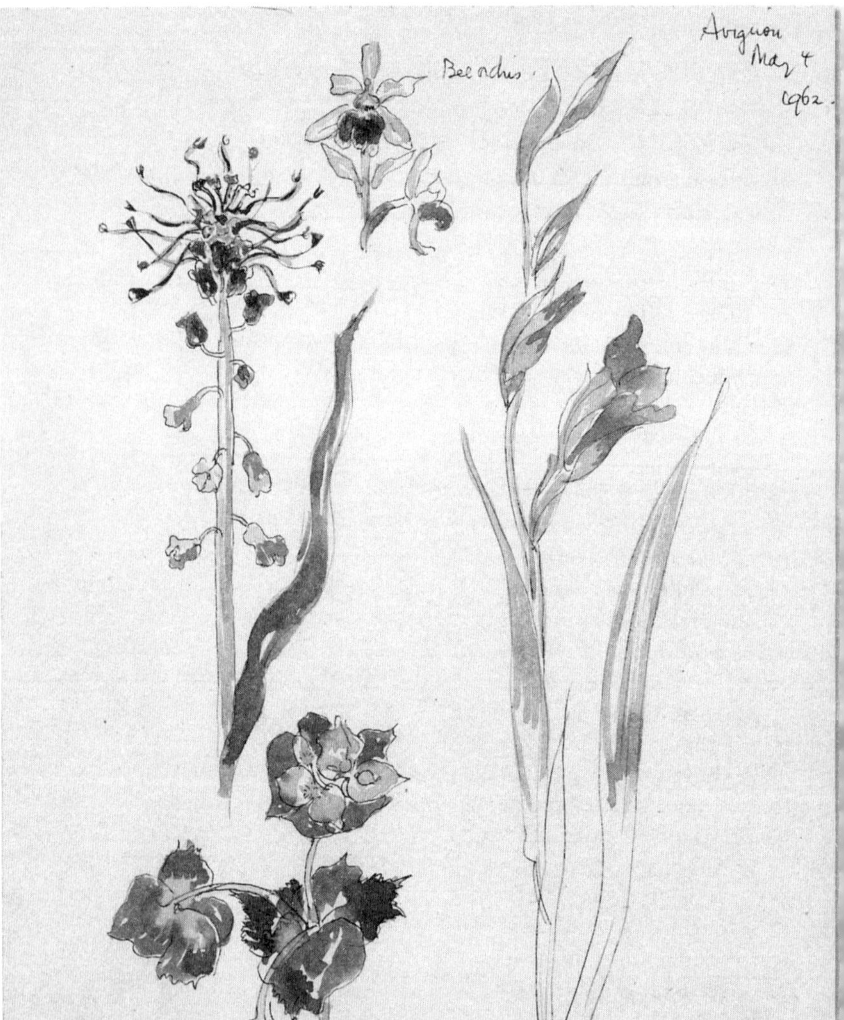
Avignon
May 4
1962.
Bee orchis.
wild gladiolus.
Tasselled Spurge

'On Prayer'

Until 1970 Joyce never revealed in public that she was a Christian Scientist. After that she was invited by all denominations to give talks in their churches and write for their magazines. This 1976 article for Catholic Life explains how she put her faith into practice.

'Pray without ceasing,' it says in the Bible (1 Thes. 5:17). What does that mean? Get down on your knees and stay there? Not as I see it.

For me prayer is not petitioning, not asking God to change anything, it is grateful acknowledgment of all the good God has already done, continues to do and continues to be; and in finding the place (the consciousness) where experience of His limitless provision of good is reality.

I believe this reality is where His children, you and I, spiritually made 'in His image and likeness' already belong. The human 'me', with my limited sense and frailty, is not this image, but the spiritual likeness is the true identity of each one of us, and prayer is acknowledgement of this likeness; and of our inseparability from God.

Why do I pray? To be aware of what God has ordained made perfect and is carrying out. Praying is being open to the power of His love, His truth and His life. 'His is the Way' (John 4:6) and His teaching says 'There is none good but one, that is God.' (Matt. 19:17); 'I can of myself do nothing' (John 5:20). Nor can we.

I find as I turn to acknowledge through spiritual discernment, what God has already done, I find answers to problems. This kind of praying is done where I happen to be, on or off my knees, day or night, in a bus, a bath, in crowds or alone.

I think that what I mean by discernment is illustrated in this anecdote: A small boy was asked: 'What do you think God is?' He paused before he answered, 'God isn't a think, He's a feel.'

One of my favourite commands in the Bible is, 'Be still and know that I am God' (Psalms 46:10). It does not tell us to be still and hope, it says be still and *know*. A comforting certainty lies behind that command; it *is* possible.

There is a great hunger, perhaps as never before, for a sense of reliable harmony in a world where the opposite is so noisily and cruelly evident. And that is putting it mildly. I find it is a practical help in any situation, and not only for myself, to realise and be able to feel that God's harmony is always going on even when it appears to be hidden by our mistakes, limited by our view and the material evidence is to the contrary.

Thus prayer, for me, is acknowledging (not as whistling in the dark but as realistic understanding) the presence of God's harmony. It helps me to find an actual sense of what spiritual reality is: ' The kingdom of heaven is at hand' (Matt. 10:7). Not a think but a feel.

I was once stuck in a lift. My companion, terrified, turned pale and looked desperate. I don't much like being stuck in lifts either, but my overwhelming desire at that moment was to relieve her great fear and, as you may have noticed, when someone else is afraid it can make one braver! I said, 'Wherever we are, we are always in the same place – whether we are in a lift, on or under ground, in the air, on or in the sea, in or out of buildings.' By which I meant that as the spiritual child of God one can never, for a fraction of a second, be outside His encompassing Love.

The lift moved, came down, and we went on our ways. Some years later I met the same girl and she thanked me for what I'd said that day in the lift. She had found it useful ever since. 'What did I say?' I asked, for I had no recollection of the day. 'Wherever we are, we are always in the same place.' I was glad she'd reminded me.

I know God had not singled me out to receive a good idea when it was needed, for His supply of good ideas is infinite and always available to everyone. That day in the lift an idea was needed and it was supplied and shared. Prayer (my desire to help) was answered in acknowledgment of God's unending love. I believe all good ideas, and indeed all good in whatever form it appears, is evidence of God's presence.

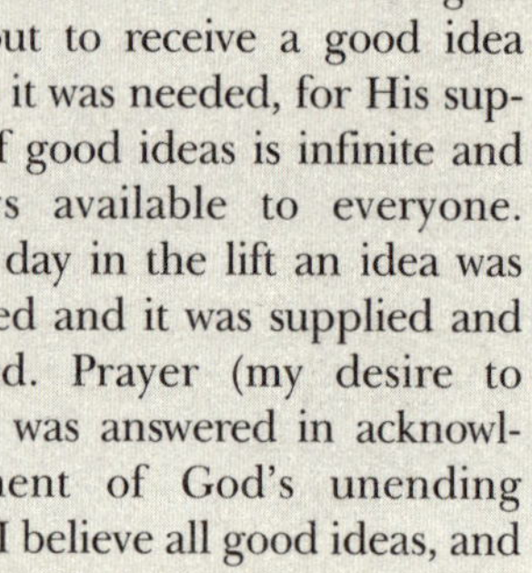

JOYCE'S FAVOURITE PLACES

One of Joyce's favourite places was Cumbria. She and Reggie stayed in Loweswater Valley every May where they pursued their shared hobby of bird watching. Reggie would identify the birds while Joyce either drew them, or wrote about them.

'Bliss'

Funny-looking in an oilskin fishing hat
I know a simple bliss on this wet day.
I am watching a pied flycatcher feed
Its invisible young above my head
In a small, dark hole high in an oak tree.
I am in a steep grove of mountain oaks
Where the sloping ground is carpeted close
In deeply springing cross-stitch patterned moss.
I am alight with the discovery
Of a small pied bird going in and out
Of a small dark hole high in an oak tree.
Rain filters through the jigsaw-puzzle leaves
As limp as silk. The air is fresh and sharp
With scents of mould and mosses, I can see
New ferns unfurling, bliss is a strong world
Wiping out all else. I know a simple bliss
Watching all this, and a bird in a tree.

1975

'A Moment with Tennyson'

his song was vritten by oyce and her irst cousin licholas Phipps or the revue enny Plain in 951. A parody n the popular ictorian song Come into the arden Maud' y Tennyson, oyce wore hite net loves and a demure dress copied from the portrait of her randmother painted by John Singer Sargent.

Maud won't come into the garden.
Maud is compelled to state
Though you stand for hours
In among the flowers
Down by the garden gate.
Maud won't come into the garden
Sing to her as you may –
Maud says she begs your pardon
But she wasn't born yesterday.

Maud's *not* coming into the garden
Thanking you just the same.
Though she looks so pure
You can be quite sure
She's onto your little game.
Maud knows she's being damping –
(And how damp you already must be)
But Maudie is now decamping
To her lovely hot-water B.

You couldn't really seriously think that
Maud is going to be such a sucker as to come into the garden.
Flowers set her teeth on edge.
And she's much too old for a strangle-hold
In a prickly privet hedge.
Pray stand while your arteries harden
It won't do the slightest good.
Maud is NOT coming into the garden,
And you're mad to have thought she would!

Notes on East Anglia

Joyce was in East Anglia on Boxing Day in 1963 when she wrote this. She said it is not a poem, but notes for a verse.

A winter walk in Norfolk
A rare day with no wind.
A great sail of sky
Spread wide over empty winter fields.
Sun: so every berry shines
In startling red
In the etched hedge
Above the bleached sedge
Pale as raw silk
Edging the sandy track.
Pheasants and a dog have walked this way
And left their print.
A tractor's giant tread
Goes arrowing on and up
Across a bicycle's bracelet
Swinging its way erratically.

Bullfinch, chaffinch, robin
Flash their winter pink
From bush to bush
Across the track,
Bright in the dustless light.

At the top of the hill
A hundred heavy weighted pigeons
Seem to be hurled
Off the stubble field
Into a row of bare-boned trees,
And sit there
Like a picture painted by a peasant.
Big fat birds all facing the same way
In big bare trees.

The sun begins to drop
Behind the red-brown elms
And all the birds are pink
Seagull, lapwing, sparrow, thrush and lark
As pink as roses
In a glowing world
Of huge pink skies, pink fields,
And rows of cottages
With fire pink eyes.

'The Sight and Sounds of Seasides Long Ago'

When I was a child the most potent kind of light was the dazzling, salt-smelling wonder of seaside light. (I know that light doesn't smell but the combination of ozone and sun-haze made a whole.)

In my selective memory it was always fair weather for the journey as my young brother and I puffed along the branch line on the Kentish coast in a soot-smelling slow-stopping train. A derelict windmill was the sign I always looked for, when it came into view we got down from the string-mesh rack our buckets and spades and my shrimping net. Any minute now, over rolling fields of long grasses blowing in the inevitable seaside breeze, we would have our first sight of the amazing sea. There, where we had left it a year ago, was the dreamed of pale blue sea. The sea – the SEA!

I was eight and full to bursting with anticipation of a repeat pattern of previous times by the sea. The feeling of rough stones under the soles of my thin sand-shoes as we picked our way from the top of the beach, through sharp sea-grasses that pricked my bare legs, to the soft white sand. There I took off my sand-shoes and felt the pleasure of cold sand between my toes. Then I ran. Lurching through the soft sand to the hard-packed proper beach sand, damp from the outgoing tide. And stood and sighed with satisfaction. It was as good as I had remembered. All that glorious space to move and play in.

We didn't know the freedom of sun and salt air on the skin for we didn't strip off on the beach. A small girl wore a cotton vest, a strange contrivance misnamed a Liberty bodice, petticoat (sometimes two, one flannel one cotton) and knickers under the cotton frock. Before I was allowed to paddle and dig canals I had to put on paddling drawers. These were bib-fronted voluminous rubber knickers into which my skirt and petticoat were stuffed. This produced a pantaloon look and was uncomfortable. Since it was all part of seaside life I didn't mind the rubbery smell.

Because of extra strong violet-rays beside the sea it was decreed that all children should wear hats. Mine was made of white cotton and was tethered by elastic under the chin. This, too, was uncomfortable because the elastic was too tight, but we were told not to fuss. None of us was allowed to bathe until two hours after our last meal. We donned our unisex, one-piece bathing-dresses, dark blue, bordered at the neck and around armholes in white that soon ran blue after contact with salt water. At first I wore a bath cap with a frill, very cissy it was. But as I graduated from squealing in the shallow waves to swimming a little with one foot on the bottom I was given a red rubber bathing cap that folded flat. It was hell to put on because the rubber was stiff and to do the job efficiently it had to fit tightly, mine pulled up my eyebrows into a position of surprise. It too smelled powerfully of rubber.

Our time in the water was strictly controlled. Some of us tended to turn blue if left in too long. Not me; I like cold water and am a glower, but I, too, had to come out when summoned. 'Come on out ... you've had enough.' I hadn't, but it was no good arguing.

Even as a child I was a people-watcher and I spent happy times on the beach watching and inventing stories about the families I saw. Sometimes, bravely, I spoke to other little girls who, like me, were shell collecting. (Boys collected seaweed ropes, dead crabs and starfishes; they also splashed us when we were all in the sea together. They didn't, then, appeal to me.) 'Have you found any cowrie shells?' was a useful opener. Cowries were the most prized shells on our beach. We put our heads together to inspect each other's findings, and thus beach-friendship began. 'What's your name?' 'How old are you? Will you be here tomorrow?' 'Oh Good.'

Of all the people to watch it is the children I find the most rewarding. I once watched a little boy about four years old. Absorbed in examining a razor shell, first from a standing position. Then he crouched down to look at it more closely; picked it up and finally, with it in his hand, he stood up still regarding it with intense concentration. Then he flung it away.

I like the very small child who isn't quite sure she likes the sea but can't resist going towards it, runs unsteadily into the first wavelet – turns to see whether there is help at hand just in case – laughs, half glee, half doubt – and runs back from the incoming foam-edged spread of water. She does this over and over again until she dares to stand still and allow the wave to break over her brown toes. It is a moment of triumph.

There were no ice-cream vendors, no donkeys or Punch and Judy shows on our beach. But we drew enormous pictures with the points of our metal spades on the hard sand. It was a status symbol of maturity to have a metal spade. We long-jumped, ran races, played rounders. And we sat for ages smoothing the sand on either side of where we had settled and after a time I wandered off with my new beach-friend. 'Don't go too far – we'll be going home soon.'

This was the last article that Joyce ever wrote, and was published just a few days after she died in 1979.

Joyce aged nine (left) with her cousins at Sandwich, Kent, 1919

In his address at the thanksgiving service for Joyce at Westminster Abbey on 7 February 1980, the Rev. Geoffrey Howard White said:

God gave talents generously when Joyce was born – she knew they came from God and worked hard to develop them. Joyce could make us laugh, cry and laugh again – all without one cruel, unkind, or unclean word or thought. She could draw, paint and compose: her records will be played, her films remembered. She was the most spiritually-minded person I have ever met.

Joyce's favourite quotation was from the English Quaker and the founder of Pennsylvania, William Penn:

And life is eternal and love is immortal, and death is only a horizon. And a horizon is nothing save the limit of our sight.

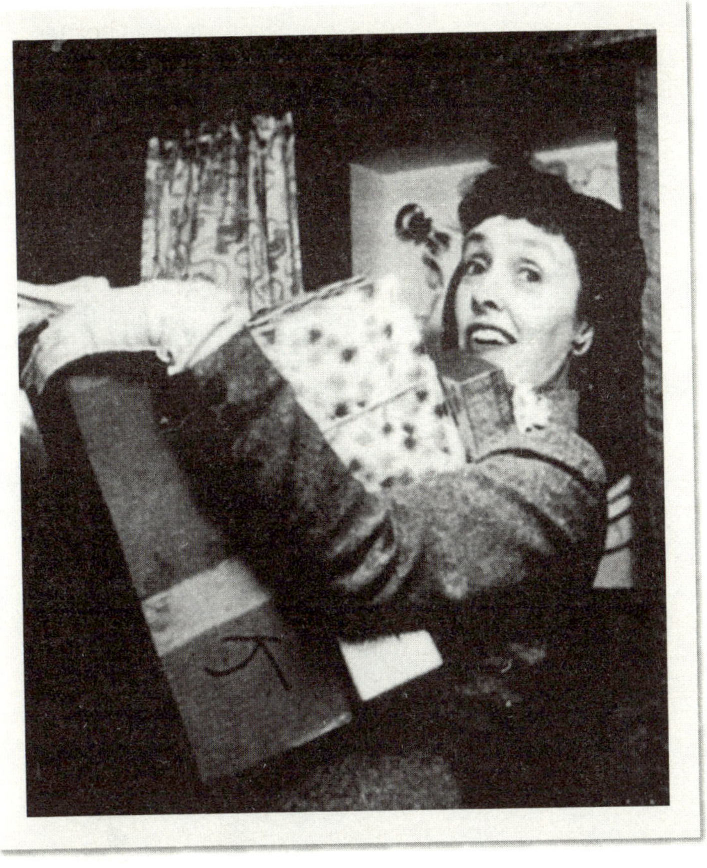

Joyce carries her Christmas
shopping home from New York on
the Queen Mary, 1957

Acknowledgments

The editor and publisher wish to thank the following for permission to reproduce material: The Estate of Stephen Potter; The Estate of J.C. Trewin; Telegraph Group Ltd; the *Observer*; *The Christian Science Monitor*; The Estate of Virginia Graham; Joan White for Rev. Geoffrey Howard White's sermon; and Claremont Fan Court School, Surrey. Illustrations and photographs courtesy of Verily Anderson, Claremont Fan Court School, James Fox, Donald Swann Estate and Leon Berger, and John Ward R.A.